# ENDORSEMENTS

"Tom is one of my 'Chosen' 7 billion special humans. Although I didn't actually read *Spiritual Choices: Putting the HERE in Hereafter*, I know what he is thinking. I support Huening's focus on the present life I have given you all. I too dislike the dogma humans have concocted since my last known prophets. I suggest (no pressure here) that you buy this book and see for yourself."

**God**
Author (ghost written) of *All the Great Spiritual Works Since Time Immemorial*

"Tom Huening is a multifaceted individual and shares many interesting ideas in *Spiritual Choices*."

**Deepak Chopra**
Author of *Life After Death: The Burden of Proof*

"I've read *Spiritual Choices* and enjoyed it. Although my favorite 'ism' is capitalism, which I consider the ultimate spirituality, I learned some things interesting to me. I recommend Tom Huening as a promising new author with a clear sense of emerging spirituality."

**Ken Fisher**
Forbes Columnist, Founder and CEO of Fisher Investments, and Author of the New York Times Bestseller, *The Only Three Questions That Count*

"Tom Huening is working in that place into which the Christian Church needs to move. He faces the issues openly and honestly and offers us *Spiritual Choices*. I recommend his work."

**John Shelby Spong**
Author of *Jesus for the Non-Religious*

"*Spiritual Choices*… is a shocking, disgusting attack on revered Catholic dogma carefully rationalized over the centuries since St. Peter assumed the mantle of Perpetual Pope-ism. Buying this book could be a matter for Confession."

**Pope Kahanus I**
Author of *Our Way or the High-Way*


"Tom Huening's *Spiritual Choices* asks, What would Moses, Jesus, Muhammad, Confucius or Buddha say today about how humans can act more human? The answers suggest how to be spiritual in a meaningful way HERE today."

**Warren Blank, Ph.D.**
President of The Leadership Group Author of *The 108 Skills of Natural Born Leaders*


"Huening suggests that evolution is real and denies that God placed fully-formed humans in the Garden of Eden 6,000 years ago. He claims contradictions in the Holy Bible and suggests being born once is enough. *Spiritual Choices*… is clearly the work of the devil. Don't read it if you ever plan to run for national politics."

**RIGHT Reverend Pat Robason**
Cathedral of the Immaculate Deception
Author of *Born into a Second Childhood – Paying the Price of Redemption*


"Relatively speaking, Huening has a good grasp of God, considering his total lack of scientific evidence. I say treat *Spiritual Choices: Putting the HERE in Hereafter* as a reasonable starting thesis and help advance our knowledge of the universe."

**Alfred Einsteen**
Author of *God is Faster Than Light*


"*Spiritual Choices: Putting the HERE in Hereafter*, the movie, is even better than the book. The action is nonstop, and the plot twists and turns. Our nomination for the Hollywood Spirit Award, we give it Five Stars!"

**Mitch Juggart**
Publisher, Rolling Rocks

# SPIRITUAL CHOICES

## Putting the *HERE* in Hereafter

**Tom Huening**

Spiritual Choices Publishing

Published by
Spiritual Choices Publishing, San Mateo, California
www.SpiritualChoices.com

Printed in the United States of America

ISBN: 978-0-9817341-2-5

Library of Congress Control Number: 2008903994

FOR CLARENCE AND HERMINA

And Special Thanks
to My Loving Extended Family


In loving memory of Donna Marie and D'Anne

# ACKNOWLEDGMENTS

Here's to all the great minds who paved the way with their thinking and writings about God, religion, and spirituality over the ages. See some of my favorites at www.spiritualchoices.com. Thank you all.

I'm grateful for the thoughts of Denise and I appreciate the pre-editing and valuable feedback from my daughter Jennifer, brother Ted, and his wife Maries; and to brother Paul for Baha'i info; and to brother Vince for his excellent suggestions.

My daughters Monica, Melissa, and Natalie, as well as friends Jessie and Huntley and all of my family, have shared unique perspectives which have added richness and color to this book.

Many other folks contributed deeply held and private beliefs about their spirituality and the choices they've made. Thank you; and your names have been changed to protect your privacy unless you chose otherwise.

Special thanks to my second printing editor Susan Shankle and her great attention to detail.

The cover is my close-up photo of a live California Bristlecone Pine. It was a seedling when Moses walked the earth. Semi-pro Bob Adler gets photo editing credit for helping me make it look good.

# TABLE OF CONTENTS

# INTRODUCTION

Can you picture little Tommy sitting in a classroom in Saint Mary's Grammar School, Des Plaines, Illinois? In the big red-brick schoolhouse, Sister Roman Marie is presiding over fifty-five fidgety first graders. It is early September and the year is 1947.

A sort of primitive fear and awe still prevail in this Catholic micro-society, six millennia after the "real" Adam and Eve. Thunder and lightning continue to invoke fear in nature, but these fears pale compared with the horrors of the skin-scorching fires of hell imagined by these six- year-olds.

Just two years before, youngish Sister Roman graduated from the Convent of Veiled Tears in nearby Chicago. Having been well versed in nun-sense and theo-magic, she has been be-cloaked in black robes, her face encased in white starched linen. She looks pained and constrained, yet radiant and confident.

Sister Roman assures us trepid students that by saying and believing her magic words, we can avoid becoming crispy critters deep in the earth's basement BBQ, called *Hell*, or its associated bun warmer, Purgatory.

Classroom discipline must be one of her favorite subjects because the first lesson we learn is that she is GOD's DIRECT REPRESENTATIVE. She asks the questions and we answer exactly as instructed:

Q: "Why did God make you?"
A: "God made me to know Him, to love Him, and to serve Him in this world, and to be happy with Him forever in the next."
Q: "Who tells us all we ought to know about God?"
A: "The Catholic Church tells us all we ought to know about God."

The good sisters of the Order of Saint Francis taught us religiously (how else?) from the *Baltimore Catechism* primer. Learning was by rigid rote, and the rewards were picture holy cards. The thorough indoctrination process

1

was scrupulously monitored by the parish pastor, the Reverend Father Bird. With his silver-white hair halo, Father Bird somehow appeared even closer to God than did the nuns. According to our God interpreters, being happy in this temporal life on earth was somewhat suspect, and certainly suspect was happiness that came from (gasp!) bodily pleasures.

The world, according to The Bird and his flock of nuns, was divided into Catholics and semi-human, non-Catholics (composed mostly of assorted other Christians). A further, lowlier level of non-Catholics was a species of quasi-humans called *pagan* (as in, "eat the crusts of your sandwich, or the pagans in Africa/China/India will starve"). We learned that heaven, hell, and purgatory, with its antechamber called *limbo*, were somehow actual physical places. Being baptized Catholic, saying your prayers (including little prayers the nuns called *ejaculations*—I swear), and avoiding mortal sins pretty much guaranteed a future abode in stratospheric Heavenly Acres.

Second grade with Sister Rosella meant preparing for and receiving First Holy Communion—the original Real Thing. Physically drop the Communion wafer host, and redemption became immediately doubtful for you, your children, and your children's children. Daily Mass service in the consecrated, converted bowling alley was mandatory, except in the case of death—your own. And it was "no laughing, no talking, no showing your teeth," in Latin or any other language during the service. Kneel down, shut up, and absorb some Grace. "And we know what you are thinking. Boys, keep your hands out of your pockets. We know what you are doing."

This indoctrination pattern has persisted since antiquity: convert some early adapter adults, and then teach the children in schools much like St. Mary's. The language we grow up with at home, along with all our familial religious beliefs, are usually carried on without question (except during that brief anti-devout time call the teenage years). By adulthood, folks typically have so much invested in their born-into religion that they have given up any thought of questioning their beliefs. They see religion as part of their personality—who they are. Few realize, at this point, they have the ability to choose a different spiritual path.

Over the centuries, faith leaders have invented doctrines and rituals that make them and their followers supposedly different and exclusive. Ever since Moses got sick on a ham hock in the desert, it was no pork for the Jews. Muslims must wash their faces five times a day, needed or not (very few zits in the Arab world). Hindus abstain from beef, especially holy cow. Not eating meat on Friday was a big Catholic deal as I was growing up. Nobody ever successfully indicted the fish lobby. But we all had our suspicions.

Some of these religious customs and rituals had practical reasons many, many years ago. Most were intended to support the tribe identity and eliminate choice. To renounce those doctrines or rituals meant social or even physical exile from tribe, clan, or family. Today the traditional rituals and doctrines, as well as a variety of new ones, act as markers of exclusivity and differentiation. They discourage choice because a change in religion means giving up the existing comfortable and familiar traditions. You might cop a plea and get excommunicated or exiled in Christianity. In Islam you could pay with your life. No major religion supports or encourages choosing a competing religion. Christianity, Islam, and Judaism don't advocate evaluating or analyzing their proprietary beliefs to facilitate your alternate spiritual choice.

You may have noted, and correctly so, that 1947 was a very long time ago. You may be wondering how and why I got to a point in my life that I would invest the energy to write a book about religion. Me, too.

I believe the seed was planted one Sunday in the early 1970s in a Catholic Church in San Jose, California. I was about thirty years old, which meant I was attending my fifteen hundredth or so consecutive Sunday Mass.

I was sitting near the front row and listening to my fifteen hundredth or so consecutive sermon, when it hit me. I was an alien. I was a stranger in a strange land. I didn't belong. Why, I wondered, are we here worshiping God? God doesn't need worship. God doesn't need anything. Don't we all agree that God is perfect, all-powerful, all-loving and all- forgiving? Who or what are we worshiping?

I found myself carrying on an internal dialogue, or rather an internal argument, with the priest delivering the sermon. I don't remember his words, but I do remember bristling at the innocent, unconscious arrogance of this priest struggling to explain the two thousand years of dogma that had been overlaid on the simple message of a holy man.

I was having a mystical experience. I'm surprised I didn't cry out. It was my come-to-Jesus meeting, and it ultimately excluded and dismissed the very church that anointed itself to interpret his words. I felt born-again to the simple words of Jesus, and simultaneously found myself dearly departed from the Catholic Church.

Only much later did I realize I had been born-again to the words of *all* of the great prophets and dearly departed from *any* institutional church.

I felt guilty, of course, and at the same time, free at last. I never again seriously attended a religious service. Oh, I have been to church services since then, but really only to confirm my de-epiphany or for the sake of curiosity. Just recently I visited the Montreal Catholic Basilica to witness a high Mass. I was struck anew at the extravagance in architecture, ceremony, and pomp. What *would* Jesus say? I pictured him knocking over the gold cups and smashing the ornate incense burner and distributing the collection money to the poor outside in the neighborhoods.

Yet I was inspired by the five-story decorated domes and the exquisite stained glass and castle-like altar, with its spires and turrets. The silk vestments, the procession of three priests, gold cross held high, and the entourage of perhaps twenty attendants were awesome. But, again, what would Jesus say?

Jesus might have been less chagrined to see what I saw a few weeks earlier in a simple village church near Antigua, Guatemala. Probably built by the Spanish missionaries, even this church with hard wooden kneelers would have seemed strange to a barefoot Jesus. Most likely, on that particular Sunday morning, Jesus would have been wandering the barrios of nearby Guatemala City, ministering to the prostitutes and hung- over drunks, and feeding the poor.

But I can empathize with the early followers of Moses, Jesus, Muhammad, or the Buddha. How does one build a sustaining community to honor and perpetuate the profound message of one's holy founder? I guess you first meet in believers' homes, then build a church as the membership expands. And as the organization grows and prospers, you build a bigger, more impressive church or temple or mosque. And then you build a cathedral. And eventually, at some point, you think you need a government, such as the Vatican, to run the whole thing.

So I've had thirty some years to think about what these holy founders would do today, how they would make religion different from religion as we know it. In short, I believe they all would do now what they did then. They would act to eliminate human suffering and injustice. They would act to help men and women become freer to choose to be more human. They would show us once again how to be compassionate and forgiving and grateful. They would show us how organized religion has strayed from their simple and profound messages. And they would redirect us toward spiritual choices aligned with their ageless messages.

So what does that mean for us today—we who want to be spiritual in a meaningful, here-and-now way, who seek to end injustice and oppression and make this a more human world?

Well, for me, it has meant learning more about what religion really means in our day and age, figuring out how we got to our worldwide religious impasse, and then writing this book.

My intent is not to insult anyone or to dissuade anyone from dearly held religious beliefs. This book is for those spiritual seekers who have questions and perhaps doubts they've been afraid to ask the religious establishment. It is for those who no longer believe in an old, bearded male God lounging above the clouds—or in a devil in hell, deep in the bowels of the earth. It is also for those who sense they might be able to lead meaningful day-by-day spiritual lives without the need for any particular religion.

Think of this book as a painting, the Sistine chapel by Michelangelo, for example, except as a paint-by-numbers watercolor. The main lines were drawn as long ago as eight thousand years, by prophets and holy men. The color numbers were added, first in bold outlines, and then segmented thousands of times by religious followers and hosts of holy hierarchies. Think church bureaucracies. We know the prophets and holy heroes created a masterpiece. We need now to scrape away the phony layers of doctrine, dogma, and ritual, and restore the original essence. This, I believe, will allow us to make spiritual choices in ways we may never have considered possible.

# YOUR SPIRITUAL CHOICES

*Church, government, or family may choose—or you can decide your
own spiritual path.*

We live in a largely secular world. We live in a mostly religious world. Yes, both. Nearly everyone identifies with a religion but leads a very secular life. We focus time and energy on daily activities: spouse, kids, work, weekends, shopping, football, and sex. Not necessarily in that order.

Yet we call ourselves Christians, Jews, Muslims, or whatever. For most of us, our designated religion is, well, a designation. We know what we grew up with. We attend services weakly (sic), monthly, or annually, and don't give it much thought. If we think about religion at all, it's due to some unusual or shocking event. Cassius Clay and some Black Panthers convert to Islam. That's odd. The Beatles get into Transcendental Mediation. How quaint. Pope John XXIII acknowledges other forms of Christianity. How nice. Protestants and Catholics kill each other in Ireland. Too bad. Jews and Palestinians kill each other in the Mid East. Nothing new here.

Then 9/11 and the World Trade Center came crashing down, our modern-day Pearl Harbor wake-up call. Who would do such a thing? Why us? What did we do to them? What could drive a group of humans to such a heinous act? They were Muslim terrorists. What's a Muslim? Are they all violent, is that part of their religion?

No, we didn't have it coming to us. Yes, religion did play a role.

And that role has been unfolding for the past half century, if not longer. Many in this country and Europe wrote off religion in the fifties and sixties as superstition and myth. Quite a few rediscovered it with a passion in the eighties and nineties. Some folks turned inward to a personal, liberating spirituality. Some went back to the literal fundamentals. The literalists sought simpler days, when they had felt secure knowing a just

God was watching over and guiding (only) them. Others of us took a hike on all things spiritual.

A very different spiritual evolution took place in many Muslim countries. There, people felt the broader cultural and economic world passing them by. They recalled the Crusades and Western imperialism, and bristled from real or imagined insults to their national pride and sometimes their religion. Encouraged by Saudi Wahhabi extremists, and indoctrinated in the fundamentalist *madrasas*, a generation grew up focused on regaining the glory of Islam. Their mission was to kill infidels. On 9/11, the nineteen perpetrators made suicidal and homicidal "spiritual" choices.

This book is about the everyday personal choices we make on our spiritual paths, and the consequences of those choices. It also examines the consequences of not making our own choices and of defaulting to what the extremists are trying to determine for us. It asks you to take a long, hard look at your own choices—what they are, how you made them, and how satisfied you are with them.

Religion seems to bring out the best and worst in people. From what I've observed, extremes in religious beliefs rarely benefit us and at worst can inflict great bodily harm. The religious fringes fervently believe they have been delegated by God to make *our* spiritual choices. More accurately, they don't believe in choice at all. Theirs is a world of commandments, directives, and orders from God. Their mission is to convert us—you and me—to their spiritual path, the one specified to them by God.

Hardly a person alive wants to hand over to someone else the power to make his or her personal choices. But not making those choices for ourselves may be a way of unconsciously ceding those choices to others. Not voting is an example, a secular one. Giving up our right or duty to vote, in essence, gives the choice to others who do vote. Not weighing in on a school or community issue means our voice is not heard. Sometimes it is hard to imagine that our choice counts, but the closer to home the issue is—the more personal it is—the more meaningful it is to us. Spiritual preferences are very close to home.

Perhaps spiritual choices may not seem very pressing to some people because, according to their religious tradition, the consequences won't play out until a "next" life. (The prophets focused on the HERE; the cleric interpreters focused more on the hereafter.) It is hard to get excited about something that might be decades, even as much as a century, away. However, as I see it, spirituality is about what is happening right here and right now. Today. Tomorrow. This life… and only much more remotely, the hereafter.

Unfortunately, we tend not to worry about our freedoms—our civil rights, legal rights, and especially religious rights—until they are threatened or our ability to choose is taken away. We finally focus only when we are forced to look at what is happening right now, in the present moment. Looking back at the history of government and religious domination, it's clear how fragile our rights are. They tend to be like muscles. If we don't exercise them, sooner or later we lose them.

Threats to freedom have been ever present over the centuries, but the threats to religious freedom in the world today are of seismic proportions. The tectonic plates of world religions have shifted and continue to grind away, enlarging the vast fault lines between world religions. Elements both within Christianity and within Islam believe theirs is the *only* way. Benedict XVI recently indicated that even being Christian is not sufficient: one needs to be Catholic to ensure salvation. Senior Muslim clerics have endorsed violence against infidels; that is, against all non-Muslims and against many non-conforming Muslims as well. These are dangerous times for personal religious freedom. For personal spiritual choices.

Despite what such radicals believe, we surely know we are not going to change others' choices or behaviors (at least not without force). That leaves us to change ourselves. What's to change? First we need to realize we can make decisions. We do have the freedom of choice. We decide where to live, where to work, who we will befriend (who we will be-enemy), and how to spend our free time. Whenever we don't decide, someone decides for us or we decide by default—that is, we decide by not deciding.

When it comes to religion, many of us decide not to decide. We are identified with the religion (or non-religion) into which we were born: Christian, Muslim, Jewish, Buddhist, Hindu, atheist, agnostic, or other. Most us passively accept the designation by our family or others and simply take our religion as a given. We tend to view it the same way we view being born white, black, tall, short, or blond. But really we do have choices. We can stay, leave, grow, shrink… or merely continue to decide by not deciding.

One restraint against embracing our given faith or any other organized religion is the checkered history of all religions. Nothing is likely to look one hundred percent appealing; the choices may not look any better than what we already have. We may conclude no religion is without sin, and therefore none is justified "to cast the first stone." So we tacitly accept our imperfect, born-into religion and wind up doing nothing.

No religious choice is perfect. Christians, Muslims, and all faiths have skeletons in the closet. Christians persecuted Jews, Muslims, and others throughout history. Think Crusades and the Inquisition. Muslims spread their faith through conquest and the sword. Missionaries work even today imposing "better" religion on "pagans" everywhere. All faiths have their own friends and enemies. Sometimes it's hard to tell them apart.

You will discover here how religions have distorted some of their original beliefs, while holding true to other beliefs. The result is a complex mixture of truth and bias. This is the case on the grand scale of world religions, and also the case for each of us personally. As you read, I encourage you to recall what you personally hold dear about your religion, as well as to examine from where your beliefs and biases have come.

You say you didn't grow up with biases? If you really have no biases, you grew up in a vacuum. Think about it.: Did you ever call a football pile up an (African American) pile when you were a kid? Did you call Brazil nuts (African American) toes? What did you call trying to bargain for a lower price? What did you call people of other religions? What did you call the mentally ill or physically disabled? Do you consider *non-Christian* or *non-Catholic* biased terms?

The important question, as I see it, is whether we are willing to look with an open mind and open heart at our own choices. We need to make our spiritual choices both consciously and intelligently, exercising our free will, yet not shying away from commitment.

Modern day gurus counsel us to find peace within. We turn to yoga, work, exercise, alcohol or drugs to try to discover security. We search continually for the absence of risk and pain. We make and spend money—in the latter cases, often money we don't have. We surround ourselves with the transitory pleasure of material things. We distract ourselves with trivial things, not just for entertainment, but also to fill a void. We ask ourselves, is this all there is to life?

For anyone who has ever questioned his or her faith; for anyone who has wondered how the miracles and far-fetched myths of religion could possibly be true; for anyone who needs more than the fantasy stories of his or her childhood faith—there is an alternative. There are viable options. There is an adult approach to understanding the mysteries of our spiritual nature. It's called *making spiritual choices* in our daily lives. These are *our* choices—your choices and my choices.

Making informed choices requires that we have information at our command. Most of us have some background in religion. But our knowledge tends to be not deep and definitely not broad. Where religion is studied, it frequently is from an exclusive and narrow point of view. In the extreme, Islamic madrasas and Christian fundamentalist schools might better be described as schools of indoctrination. Even in the mainstream public education domain, few schools offer "comparative religion" courses because of negative political and social pressures. Thus, one of the greatest influencers of our entire civilization is given short shrift.

I wrote this book as a way to make up for this deficit and to help us gain some of what we may have missed.

I begin with a discussion about God and a fractured tale of Adam and Eve. Next, I describe the "initial public offerings" of some religions, followed by an analysis of some disturbingly bad choices made by institutional religions ("religion run amok"). Hopefully with minimum bias, I then summarize some known and some less well-known facts about the major world religions.

Finally, I explore some cultural values and clashes, and their consequences and outcomes in the world. I believe we do need to understand about the religious drivers of terrorism. What warped rationale led nineteen humans to target the almost three thousand innocent non-combatants in the World Trade Center towers? What bias drives Sunni Muslims to kill Shi'ite Muslims or Baha'is? What are fundamentalist Christians thinking in wishing death for foreign leaders who have beliefs contrary to their own? What causes Catholics to disown other Christians? What drives sects of all kinds to act like materialists—counter to their supposed beliefs? How can our choices make a difference to these groups, or to anyone in the world?

The subject of religion and the choices we make are critical to our cultural and spiritual survival. But this book isn't about Armageddon. I've

Tom Huening

tried to keep it a light read. Nowhere do I pretend to be a theologian or philosopher. It's more about practical common sense and what direction to go from here. It's about how to act in our own enlightened self- interest.

To actually decide a spiritual path, rather than follow one blindly or bushwhack a path of our own through the wilderness, we need to know more about the fascinating origins and history as well as the current state of religion. We need to realize that the emphasis of some religions has managed to morph from the HERE to the hereafter. More knowledge, information, and historical wisdom are always a good thing. Our inquiry can contribute a bit to a better present-day world and lead us to a profoundly more satisfying personal spirituality.

# SECTION ONE

# BEFORE ORGANIZED RELIGION

# GOD, WE KNOW YOU ARE THERE

*Humans imagine God in many, many ways.*

The question of where babies come from triggered early humans' first spiritual thoughts. Mechanics of conception and birth puzzled them. They thought God or magic created new life.

Neanderthals attributed awesome power to the sun, moon, storms, floods, earthquakes, droughts, sickness, and death—as well as birth. The gods punished or rewarded. Ancients saw a God who favored but mostly cursed.

Early humans anointed god-go-betweens to intercede with this all-powerful force. Genesis, the biblical story of creation, reminds me of one such shaman—my favorite "grandson" of the prophet Adam.

Six thousand years ago, when the earth was six days old, God created Adam from muck. God provided Adam all the comforts of home, including an enormous menagerie for company. But God saw that Adam felt lonely. No animal could nag, and so Adam found his life incomplete. Besides, the animals all did exactly what Adam ordered, and somehow that didn't seem right either. God saw that Adam longed for a soul mate.

So God slipped Adam a Mickey Finn, performed outpatient surgery to remove the best part of Adam's brain, and fashioned a clearly superior being whom He named Eve. Adam awoke, saw Eve, and thought, Great, somebody to boss around.

"God, you're the greatest," said Adam, causing Eve to ask, "Who are you talking to?"

Adam replied, "Don't worry your pretty little head about God. I'm the man and I'll translate and interpret everything God says, and it will be for your own good."

Eve answered, "Oh, thank you, big, strong, and handsome Adam," and thought, We'll see about that.

Adam and Eve liked paradise, but craved the excitement of a little mischief. Opportunity reared its head like a snake of a salesman. For no money down, he offered a candy-apple red vehicle to drive them to a place called *Truth or Consequence*. They took the bait. God, playing the premier, prototype lawyer, sued their naked butts for breach of their lease. He evicted them from the Garden of Eden.

They wandered homelessly, until stumbling upon Grog, the first real estate salesman, in the first known subdivision: East Eden Heights. Both parties recognized the limited marketplace and a school district with potential. The parties quickly consummated the deal.

Newly settled in their energy-efficient, passive-solar, cold-water loft, Eve casually remarked to Adam, "Honey, do you think granite color would go with our bear skin rug?"

Adam replied, "Sweetie, did you remember that I'm inventing golf this weekend, and that Home Depot won't open for another 5,900 years?"

"Honey, I completely forgot," replied Eve. "But, remember, you promised to arrange the boulders in the baby's room."

Adam frowned. "Tell me again: What is a baby, and where do babies come from?"

Eve explained. Then, except for those nights when she had a headache, the couple diligently worked at making babies. Doing the math, they realized the enormity of populating the world. They worried too about child care and the lack of reliable diaper service.

Soon fussy little Cain arrived, and just ten months later, darling Abel showed up to introduce the first sibling rivalry. Cain grunted to Eve, "What's this red, slimy intrusion into our idyllic three-person family, competing for my food and affection?"

"Now, Cain," Eve answered tenderly, "put that skull-crushing rock down and give Abel a gentle hug."

As young adults, farmer Cain offered a sacrifice to God in the form of a rutabaga, whereas Abel proffered a cute little lamb. Between them, which would you choose? We all know this rivalry did not turn out well. After Abel's untimely demise, Cain left the cave to move further East of Eden.

Many sons and daughters later, baby Seth arrived. Adam had just turned 130 years old (nearly six thousand years prior to Viagra). Suffice to say, before the concept of incest, the world quickly populated.

Seth's son Adamino might not be familiar to you—unless perhaps you read between the lines, as I did. However, we have reason to believe this fellow was a smart-assed prodigy. No sooner had he reached puberty at age thirteen, than he announced his calling. His declined to tend sheep or farm. Instead he interpreted and corrected all that he saw around him. He developed a specialty criticizing parental directives. Adamino, as a teen, first used the phrases "yeah, right" and "whatever."

Adamino began his prophetic mission by correcting all his parents told him. He focused particularly on what came to be known as *chores*. His parents thought his talents would be best utilized hunting mastodons, so they specifically forbade him to visit a region well beyond East Eden known now as Siberia.

The boy's parting words were, "You can't stop me! I'm outta here."

Adamino survived the cold by grubbing for grubs and field salad greens. A sympathetic mastodon family adopted him, enabling him to survive for years in the wild. Amazingly, he found his way back to East Eden Heights two generations later. Although Adam and Eve had since departed, Adamino's siblings had chronicled his banishment on the cave walls. Considering the harsh nature of his exile destination, he had long been assumed dead.

His arrival home caused quite a stir. The tribe considered him a spirit. Scissors, safety razors, and combs not yet invented, Adamino appeared as one hairy dude. And sleeping with the mastodons had created a strong aura about him. Seizing his fifteen minutes of fame, he encouraged rumors about his divinity. In this way, he assumed the mantle of the first holy/wise guy. His credentials included directly descending from his father's father, Adam.

Because he discovered religion, Adamino naturally defined its role. He invented priestly magic to sustain popular interest.

Having lived with the wild beasts, he had developed a keen sense of low-frequency hearing. He could hear the rumbling approach of thunderstorms long before those around him could. His correct rain shower predictions helped the tribe. Soon tales of his great power to intercede with the all-important rain and sun gods had spread through the land. After a while, no one cared that he didn't hunt or fish with the men. He lived off the gifts and offerings of the community. He became the first to set up a profitable business as a rain maker.

Because wild boar was his favorite food, Adamino instituted pig sacrifices to the thunder god. The roasted sacrifices mysteriously disappeared from the altar shortly after the ceremony. Adamino expanded his role. Village virgins threw themselves at his feet and at other bodily places. He became a papa many times over. Of course, he had a favorite wife/cousin and a favorite among his 123 sons. Establishing a precedent for the generations that followed, papa set up this favorite son Adamito in the miracles and prophecy business. The natives accepted this hard-of- hearing son as the most-likely-to-succeed influencer of the gods of thunder and sun.

The abridged version of Genesis, which most people read, verifies the main points of this story.

Humankind actually evolved on this planet some two hundred thousand years ago and began to establish the humble, mythical beginnings of religion. Since then, we have worshiped something or someone and have always believed in magic. Somebody, too, has always found a way to capitalize on human fears, needs, and desires to know and to please a Supreme Being. Whenever people had difficulty grappling with their spiritual choices, members of a self-anointed priestly caste were standing by, ready to make those decisions in their stead.

After Adam and his offspring multitudes, it came to be that wise guys were regarded as wise men. Wise men became low, medium, and finally high priests. (In one ancient culture they became tall, grande, and venti priests.) The occupation required organizing, marketing, and directing skills.

The major religions and faiths have storylines about the formation of the universe and the advent of man. The Bible tells how God created the world, some believe six to eight thousand years ago. God added the starry dome of the heavens. Then He created various life forms: plants, animals, and man. The various stories, many of them competing with and contradicting one another, detailed how we and the world got here. They morphed into regulations, customs, and rituals surviving today.

Gods proliferated until there was a god for everything: birth, life, death, fertility, sun, moon, war, food, and teenagers. Societies from the earliest of times honored deities. High priests scripted these gods into religious show productions. These dramas featured superstars and casts of thousands. Cecil B. would have been proud.

Whenever audience interest waned, the high priest suddenly would be blessed with a natural disaster. Yes, they fervently prayed (much like today's media) for a swarm of locusts or a drought. Then began the next plot—maybe a hut-buster hit to rekindle religious interest and/or inspire disaster preparedness. In the process, maybe they'd audition a new vestal virgin.

And so religions proliferated as quickly as populations.

Religions grew because humans needed them to explain their world. Our "loss of innocence" and awareness of good and evil came with a price. With religion came guilt, anxiety, and what Sigmund Freud called *the trauma of self-consciousness.*

Early religions and ritual beliefs helped humans cope with the pervasive anxieties of eat-or-be-eaten (the origin of fast food; namely, be fast or be food) and you're-going-to-die-soon-anyway. Worship of anything was fair game. Imagine life before recorded history; for example, life as a coyote. Larger animals will kill you if you get in their way or in the way of their dinner. As a coyote, you are faster than most beasts, but brave the danger of the hunt to eat and survive. Cold and wet weather affects you and your food supply. Forest and grass fires, disease, and many things you don't understand determine whether you live or die.

So it is no wonder that humans, with increasing levels of self-consciousness, created reasons for the events affecting their everyday lives. How can we decrease the dangers of the unknown? How do we survive another day, another week, month, or year? Powerless humans attempted to control their surroundings. They learned the fine art of god appeasement.

We came to worship the ground we walked on: mother earth and our known universe. We saw the sun cause our crops to grow or whither. If gentle, rains helped; if violent, our huts and gardens washed away and hunting became difficult or impossible.

So we worshiped all we could not control nor understand. We worshiped animals, mountains, the sun, moon, and stars as spirits who could help or harm us. Animism became religion in its earliest and least organized form. Later-day revealed religions assumed animists were savages who created false gods to allay their fears. This rejection worked both ways: earlier religions were discarded as primitive, and newer, competing religions were regarded as atheistic or heresy. If this is the case, what will future generations think of our beliefs today?

Still, today the fifth or sixth largest religious group in the U.S. is neo-pagan. They mirror early fertility religious beliefs followed by the animists.

No reliable information exists about the origins of animist or fertility religions; they began before recorded history. Humans took a while to figure out that males played a role in procreation. So early fertility worship focused on the goddess as giver of human life. Gradually, male gods horned their way in, as it dawned on men that they too had a role in generating life. Rain, sun, and power forces were male, and the moon and gentle things female. In the centuries before monotheisms developed, pagan and polytheistic religions featured multitudes of gods and goddesses—some weird and some quite good looking, at least by modern sensibilities.

Early hieroglyphics and writings tell us about these disparate and loosely organized ancient religions. Most religious customs were local, but a few were broader based and better known.

**Egyptians,** for example, devoted mega community productivity to the worship of kings, queens, and pharaohs—dead or alive. Egyptian high priests (cornering the embalming market) explained that pharaohs could live forever, thereby protecting the populace. Eternal life came by following the priests' check-out-of-life instructions. The funeral business prospered as it expanded to include the king's entire court (except the high priest, of course). The trek to the nether world became a big business. Slaves and commoners had a substantial investment in assuring the afterlife of their protecting pharaoh/gods. Egyptians spent much of their gross national product on afterlife social security.

Egyptians expressed their myriad gods first in pictures, then in words about heroic or dastardly deeds. Each god was nasty or nice, depending on his or her fears and aspirations. Pharaoh's favorite became the honcho god.

Originally thought to be born as gods, Egyptian kings exposed their warts, social diseases, and human failings. Royals reproduced like bunnies (many wives equals much courtly fooling around). So royal succession was decided, and only then did the key priest ritually transfigure the ruler into a god, in a manner much like today's partisan political convention. His god title helped the king maintain law and order.

In addition to transforming the king into a god, the priests shined statues, read religious scrolls, and generally led the good life. Surely they prayed for the king's health and vigorously discouraged the king from deciding to take priests along on the afterlife journey.

These and other duties, such as making incense and magic potions, were demanding work, so priests were supported by temple riches and granaries. When things got tough during the later dynasties, tomb robbing augmented the priests' income, often with a cut of the loot to the reigning king.

Some royalty and priests abused their power. However, Egyptian commoners were typically devout in their worship and beliefs. They opposed murder, stealing, lying, and adultery, and maintained a strong sense of justice. Through their religious beliefs, or perhaps merely because of an innate human moral sense, the people of early Egypt created and maintained an impressive civilization.

We know somewhat more about the **Greek** culture and religious practice because humans' handwriting had improved by then.

Greeks worshiped in temples that served as sacrificial barbecue altars (the sauce ingredients are still secret). The temples were dedicated to a particular god: Apollo, Eros, or the king of gods, Zeus. The Romans eventually conquered Greece, and here's why. The Greek priests and congregations ate the sacrificial animal meat, and the gods got leftover blood, skin, and bones. Oxen, horses, pigs, and sheep all fell victim to PETA (Penitents for the Eating of Tasty Animals).

Even worse for Greek men, Greek women worshiped Dionysus, the god of wine. In pursuit of libation and liberation, many of these ladies abandoned their spouses and families. They became the world's first hippies.

**Romans,** being friendly Italians, renamed and adopted many of the Greek gods. The political "big tent" theory of inclusion meant Zeus, the king of gods, was now Jupiter. This god of the skies, lord of the gods, approached the idea of a head God or a Supreme Being. Eros (who became Cupid) and Dionysus (who became Bacchus) are two modern day favorites.

Rome's elite political priest caste, the *fetial*, became intermediaries between humans and the gods, especially for ritual sacrifice. This go-between function dates back to Adamino. Kings claimed divinity or saw themselves as god descendants. A head of household or tribal elder often acted as god intermediary. Gods were too mysterious, powerful, and scary to approach without a spiritual guide. That guide, like those of the Egyptians and Greeks, could be a shaman, medicine man, or priest.

Mythology commingled with religion during early recorded history. The gods of myth had many human characteristics, including emotions, strengths, and flaws. These myth stories related adventures, love affairs, quarrels, murders, incest and intrigue, all in an effort to understand and explain the supernatural. Mythology signaled the beginnings of both organized religion and modern soap operas. *As the World Turns,* the long-running TV soap opera, dates to this period.

So why did we find it necessary to acknowledge, appease, and adore the gods—or, later, a single Divine Being—someone most could neither see nor directly sense? Surely fear played a part. Early humans had little control over their lives. Natural disasters, wild animals, harsh weather, mysterious disease, hostile humans, and early forms of income tax all threatened their survival. Our early ancestors had to look to someone to create hope for their very existence. Someone in history always helped with (or played on) their fears.

Take the case of Icarusito, the illegitimate son of the mythical boy aviator Icarus. Icky, as the son was called by his friends, grew up on the Greek island of Crete on a sheep ranch near Mt. Hellenus, overlooking the Icarian Sea. His teenage dad, along with the boy's grand-Daedalus—neither expert in aerodynamics—had fashioned seagull-feather wings glued with candle wax. Epoxies had not yet been discovered. We all know the story: Icarus, in search of god, flew too close to the sun, ignoring grand-Daed's advice. The heat melted the wax, and papa went ballistic.

Icarusito, with his legitimate mom, were left to tend their legitimate sheep and to fend for themselves. Insurance was yet to be invented, so they received no lump sum settlement (unless you count the flight wreckage).

Icarusito suffered harassment by his cruel little friends, who questioned his dad's foolish use of wax instead of low-melt olive tree resin.

Then, one morning in Novembrius in the year negative 244, Icarusito hiked up the mountain to fetch the happily grazing sheep. Depressed by the taunts of his friends and tuckered after his long trek, he rested uneasily against a lone pine tree. The sun god was hidden that day by gathering storm clouds. It rained, thundered, and a bolt of lightning struck his resting place, knocking the lad unconscious.

He awoke to the acrid smell of his Merino wool sweater, scorched in a way to suggest writing. Hurriedly, he herded the sheep home.

First his mother, then his aunt, then grand-Daed, and finally the townsfolk were all amazed at the evidence. Looking very carefully, they discerned a message burned into the back of Icarusito's sweater. Though no one in town could read, Icarusito divined that he had been commanded to take up his father's quest. He would restore his dad's scorched reputation.

Word quickly spread to nearby villages, and soon Icarusimo (as he then came to be known) had established a following. He decided that the gifts brought by admirers were a much easier way to make a living. So he gave up herding sheep, and he and his sweater hit the road. His fame preceded him. Villagers begged him to answer problems about sheep, crops, life, death, marriage, and of course, aerodynamics.

And so, again and again, as far back as we can see in history, humans have believed in myth, magic, and miracles, and they wanted to believe in God. From time's beginning, we see prophets, priests, and shamans available as guides to approach the other world. The next chapter in this fully-certified prehistory leads us through a concise examination of the beginnings of the world's great organized religions and the choices that have been made on our behalf over the centuries.

# RELIGION GETS ORGANIZED

*Could the founding prophets have realized what would become of their simple message?*

Years 800 to 200 BCE (Before Common Era) marked the beginning of fertile religious times. This six-hundred-year period saw the birth of new religions all over the civilized world. Folks became more socially aware. People realized they were being exploited and weren't well protected by the ruling class. The luster of kings and clergy diminished. Peasants moved to cities and began to feel they might have a future.

Religions traditionally claim, "We were first, so we're the best," and date their conception to the earliest possible time. But many date to the same approximate time. This suggests religions were a rational or practical response to changing social conditions. The prosperous merchant class partially caused and certainly spread the seeds of social awareness and organized religions.

As religions were born under similar social conditions, so they developed and organized along similar lines in a world where change was ubiquitous. Civilizations naturally advanced at different rates, but the patterns of growth were somewhat parallel in the population centers of the world. Once trade was widespread, social ideas and hope for the future became widespread.

By the middle of the first millennium, Christianity dominated, and its influence still covers a huge part of the world. Islam also then gained religious and political control over large sections of civilization and currently has enormous influence over many countries. Dominance by these great forces didn't leave much wiggle room for alternate viewpoints.

Folks clung to the security of literal religious beliefs during the (Western) Dark Ages, but the Renaissance introduced humanism. That changed everything. Not only did human worth exist in faith, but people began to believe they were capable of learning virtually anything. This perfectibility-of-man concept claimed that present-day life was as important as the Christian afterlife.

By this time, people commonly agreed life was the pits. In Europe, monarchies and the Catholic Church had pretty much sucked up all the wealth and power. The peasants were left with zero. Bishops and abbots often wielded controlling power. They dispensed and collected spiritual and political favors.

Then, as in the case of a modern drug deal gone bad, the clergy competed and fought about selling indulgences (pay your way out of hell). Leading the charge for reform, in 1517, Catholic monk Martin Luther nailed his famous protest to the cathedral door. He claimed indulgences were useless to sinners and corrupted the clergy. Folks read about Church corruption and Luther's intended reforms thanks to the newly invented printing press. They smelled the possibility of change.

Change did not come easily. If regular folk could read and interpret scriptures, per Luther, why did they need power-hungry, money- sucking, holy-water-pond-scum, war-mongering Church administrators? Okay, perhaps that was a bit harsh. Devout, well-meaning clergy, though, were overshadowed by the rampant abuse perpetrated at the top of the hierarchy.

So, feeling unwanted and persecuted, the Church reformed. Guess again. They turned the other cheek. Guess again. They did what self-perpetuating bureaucracies always do: they fought change. They circled the wagons and fought wars of survival. They instituted censorship, book banning, and the infamous Inquisition. The papal administration reaffirmed their power and the dogma of the Church. Actually, a bit of real reform limited political incest and expanded the education and discipline of the clergy.

Because politics and religion were so closely intertwined, those who declared themselves Protestants threatened the king as well as the Catholic Church. Maintaining religious conformity propped up the political and religious status quo. So Protestants were labeled *heretics* and charged with treason.

A generation of attempts at reform, unholy alliances, and economic bad times followed. These culminated in the 1572 St. Bartholomew Day Massacre in Paris, where Catholics attacked and killed much of the Protestant (Huguenot) leadership. (Any similarities to twentieth century Catholic and Protestant fighting in Northern Ireland are strictly coincidental.) The War of Religions that followed lasted the rest of the century. Not until 1598 were the Protestants granted limited autonomy and religious freedom. Then the Thirty Years War (1618–1648) renewed the conflict between the peace lovin', turn-the-other-cheek Catholics and Protestants.

After the religious dislocations of the Reformation (mostly during the 1500s), an entire period of European history was focused on the dawn of scientific reasoning. This, in turn, produced further major consequences for organized religion. Not all religions were affected in the same way at the same time. Because Islam and Hinduism were geographically distant from the Reformation and did not wield central control over their doctrine and dogma, scientific development had less impact on them than it had on Christianity.

William James said that, long ago, people took truth to be whatever had not yet been contradicted. Thus, Aristotle thought the power of the lever was derived from the miraculous character of the circle. Herodotus believed the cold drove the sun South in the winter. and magic was present on almost every page of cures in early medical books.

Philosophers, especially during the Enlightenment, tried to establish an irrefutable intellectual foundation, a prime or beginning assumption, upon which to base their philosophizing. Typically it was something obvious and unarguable, such as Kant's *cogito ergo sum*: "I think, therefore I am." Today we assume we exist and go get a Starbucks (which certainly exists).

In 1543, Copernicus kick-started the scientific era by saying the earth and other planets revolved around the sun. Galileo validated the theory with his improved telescope and published his *Dialogues* in 1632. He caught major Papal flack as the Church became ever more adamant the earth was the center of the universe. "That's our story and we're sticking to it," said Pope Urban VIII. Cardinal Robert Bellarmine backed up his boss, saying, "Any fool can see the sun rises in the morning and revolves around the earth. Next, Galileo will preposterously claim that Jesus wasn't born of a virgin."

Galileo's famously purported opinion? "I do not feel obliged to believe that the same God who has endowed us with sense, reason, and intellect has intended us to forgo their use."

This suggests the Catholic Church is inflexibly dogmatic. And we can speculate that Galileo, Copernicus, Leonardo de Vinci, and Charles Darwin wished that they had never opened their big, intelligent, rational mouths. However, the Vatican did ultimately agree with Galileo, and in 1822 removed his book from its banned books index. As a nice touch, 359 years late, Pope John Paul II issued a full apology for Galileo's heresy trial. Note that the reformer Luther and the Protestant hierarchy had agreed with the Catholic Church in condemning Galileo. Some fundamentalists still believe the earth and heavens were created in seven days and Adam and Eve were real people.

However, in general, people began to believe in an orderly, understandable universe beyond the world of the Bible and the Qur'an. Some suggest Newton began it all when an apple dropped on his head and he proceeded to figure out why. Isaac proposed that stuff doesn't just happen, it happens according to observable and verifiable natural laws and principles. Newton invented calculus and discovered classical mechanics.

Speculation was out. Science, math, and experimentation were in. It began to look as though we humans could know things in a way that could be organized and replicated. Newton's contemporaries got a little cocky and imagined they were "looking into the mind of God," and looking without the help of religion. The step that followed was a big one.

Some became skeptics. They said if you can't apply reason to a fact or prove it, it isn't true or doesn't exist. They applied this logic to all religion. Deism was one result. It holds God exists as demonstrated by reason and nature alone. God does not intervene in the "perfect" world He created. There is little room for miracles in this view. Deism never became an organized religion, but was a blow to organized religion then and ever more. Thus, the Enlightenment spawned an anticlerical movement, but also a strong faith in religion and intense spirituality.

People felt cautiously more independent of traditional religion. Science and reason provided new and alternate ways to find God. The notion of an individual free to make spiritual choices was formed. Scientific reasoning gave a few folks the courage to choose a path that had not been dictated or approved by the holy mother Church.

Governance in politics as well as religion was forced to change. Kings then were Church anointed. The authority of both was challenged, and the seed of liberty was planted. Government and Church began to be thought of as representatives of the people. Monarchy and clerical stock downgraded from "hold" to "sell."

The American and French Revolutions sprang, in part, from a belief in the importance of individual rights—thinking and choosing for oneself. In the U.S. Declaration of Independence, God is described as "Creator," "Nature's God," the "Laws of Nature," "Supreme Judge," and "Divine Providence," rather than as God or the Supreme Being. Before, under the dogmatic direction of monolithic Christianity, God would have been called simply *God*. But the founding fathers introduced the concept of spiritual choice. They established that we as a fledgling country would not be ruled by Rome, nor by any organized religion. Non-institutional spiritual choices were proclaimed part of the God-given freedoms of America. God was allowed to mean different things to different people.

The French Revolution resulted in re-appropriation of the Roman Catholic Church's land holdings and political influence, leaving only religious freedom of choice. Certainly, this was an improvement over the Catholic Church being in charge of all spiritual choices for everybody. In America, the founders not only guaranteed religious freedom, but went further and forever separated it from civil governance. These revolutions changed irrevocably the divine right of kings in Western cultures and ended the codependency of Christian religion and rule. Muslim countries only recently have experimented with separation of church and state, and religion and civil government remain closely tied in most cases.

Science advanced. Pasteur's experimentation with germs (1860s) shook religion like a 9.0 Richter earthquake. The wrath of God had been such a convenient motivator. A punishing God could be seen as a fair explanation for plagues, pestilence, and other ills of the flesh, considering the embryonic science of those times. Before medical science, for example, headaches were plausibly attributed to punishment for lustful thoughts, rather than—as we know now—more likely an avoidance of marital sex. Through the discoveries of science folks became inoculated against many of the threats of dogmatic hocus pocus.

Most modern world religions, including Christianity, have reconciled with science. Burnings at the stake have markedly decreased. The Catholic Index of forbidden heretical books—my teenage must-read list—disappeared. With the exception of a few flat-earth-ists, most of the world's Christians, Muslims, Jews, Buddhists, Hindus, Baha'is, and others learn from the same science news and academic sources.

People the world over accept and have become accustomed to scientific truths based on observable facts.

And so, from simple founding principles, the world's religions morphed into life-directing organizations. Judaism and Christianity began with the image of an all-controlling God. And that God evolved for some into a God who had created a perfect, rational world, and then left it to run on scientific principles. However, the watchmaker God, who wound up the universe and let it run, turned out to be too impersonal for most people. So, in the years since the Enlightenment, many have returned to the concept of a more personal, caring, and involved-in-the-details God.

We see, too, that organized religion's role in the spiritual choices of its followers has evolved over time. Religion continues to be a powerful world force and still today makes spiritual choices for most people. Still, at least in some cultures, people increasingly value the freedom to make their own choices. In free societies, we have that option, even if we don't always have the inclination to make our own spiritual choices.

Christianity and Islam, in particular, continue to press their "right and duty" to make our personal spiritual decisions—especially those decisions leading toward a promised afterlife. Why do we give them our power to choose? Do we not realize that, in this high-tech world, we have the same or better information than they have? Is it that we have lost sight of the HERE and now? Is it just that we haven't thought to decide our own spiritual future?

These are questions some may find scary to ask. Because to answer them we must take off our rose-colored glasses and look at the clear, simple truths of religion. We must be willing to see how bureaucratic, institutional religion has run amok and gone astray.

In the next section, I make the case that religions are frequently self-serving and prone to perpetuate their status and power. (Sound like politics?) Based on the abuses I lay out in the chapters that follow, you may agree that "command and control" religion is not the best spiritual chooser for you, nor for humankind.

# SECTION TWO

# RELIGION RUN AMOK

# MY RELIGION IS BETTER THAN YOURS

*Believe as you will, but your right to practice your religion ends
where mine begins.*

We like to believe our religion is the original, the only, the right path, that we are the chosen ones and our God and prophets are better than yours. If we believe in tolerance toward other faiths, it's tolerance to the extent we're willing to put up with your curious (perhaps misguided) beliefs.

Of all the forces that have shaped the civilized world, religion has been among the most powerful. In a world population in excess of seven billion, more than five billion associate themselves with an organized religion. True, many fewer practice the principles or rituals and actually *act* according to that religion; but most humans say they believe in God, in Allah, in a Supreme Being.

Some argue religion and belief in an exclusive God have been the greatest cause of evil in history. Certainly, much harm has been done in the name of God. "Worship my God, or I will overpower or kill you" is the perversion that has given religion a bad name. The founding prophet dudes typically didn't intend it that way. It happened when religion got organized.

Would the war of separation between India and Pakistan have been sanctioned by Hindu or Muslim principles? Would the Muslim conquest of Christian Spain (both Peoples of the Book) have been encouraged by Muhammad? Would Jesus have sanctioned the Crusades? What sort of God would have approved of the counter-Christian conflict in Northern Ireland between Protestants and Catholics? How about the Bosnian battle or the perennial Israeli/Palestinian struggle in the holy lands? (Again, in each case, both parties are Peoples of the Book.) Wars have always been about conquest—of the strong over the weak, of territory, or of competing ideologies.

That wars have been fought in the name of God perhaps only shows that there is no idea so noble it cannot be perverted by unscrupulous men (and some women). Unfortunately, leaders of institutional religion often have initiated or promoted the perversions.

Theologians have argued the idea of a holy war. Pairing the concept of God with human slaughter in pursuit of principle or real estate must rank right alongside ethnic cleansing as the all-time greatest oxymoron.

Self-defense might be argued as consistent with Islam, but doesn't the Qur'an say, "Do not kill each other, for God is merciful to you. If any of you does these things, out of hostility and injustice, We [God] shall make him suffer Fire: and that is easy for God" (sura 4: aya 29-30; *sura* meaning section, *aya* meaning verse).

Suicide extremists' attempts to justify mayhem through the Qur'an fail to reconcile with this passage: "Spend in God's cause: do not contribute to your destruction with your own hands, but do good, for God loves those who do good" (sura 2: aya 195).

Jesus raised havoc with the money changers in the Temple, but apparently did them no physical harm. Rather, the message of Jesus argued against even self-defense in his admonition to turn the other cheek. Note that Jesus could have hidden himself or even fought against his Crucifixion. But he did not.

Buddhists, Hindus, Baha'is—none would sanction violence, at least not according to the founders' principles and what they thought God would expect from us mortals. But religion inevitably got mixed up in politics and the human pursuit of power. Looking beyond the stories of olden times is difficult. It was those who ruled by divine right and their academic henchmen who wrote history, not the prophets or dissenters.

Historically, the king and the church became the first two major political parties. They cooperated and competed, as the situation warranted. They conspired and fought, sometimes to the death, over the spoils of control of the minds and properties of humankind.

The techniques and tools of subjugation evolved with the growth of inventions of terror, but the basic concept of maintaining control stayed the same. Attribute your source of power to a divine being whom only the priest and king can see and hear, and then suppress or kill those who didn't buy the official line.

Conquistador Cortez in Mexico in the early 1500s, with his missionary detachment, subjugated Aztec Tenochtitlan, perhaps the largest and most civilized city in the world at that time. In addition to contributing the word of Christ, he contributed smallpox, gold lust, and genocide, killing more than a hundred thousand natives. And his cousin Pizarro in Peru subjugated and brought so-called civilization to the Incas. He converted them so they could suffer and die as Christian slaves in the silver and gold mines. But they were promised a swell hereafter.

Both Cortez and Pizarro were loyal emissaries of the guardian of the Church, the crowned-by-the-Pope, Holy Roman Emperor, Charles V, the King of Spain. Charles V famously said, "To God I speak Spanish, to women Italian, to men French, and to my horse—German." Through his agents, he spoke death and destruction to the North and South American natives. And Charles had many kingly cousins in crime—before, during, and after his reign—conquering real estate and spreading their "better" religion.

Missionaries of all faiths substantially influenced the societies where they preached. They brought modernization (McDonalds nowadays), sanitation, and medical advances. Think Columbus, Cortez, and other explorers, accompanied by their missionary chaplains. When the effects of disease, enslavement, and ethnic cleansing had begun to wear off, they brought basic education and commerce. Only after the natives had been subjugated—or if necessary, eliminated—could real conversion and "reform" take place.

Proselytizing has always suggested "our God and our religion are better and stronger than yours." It was and is a not-so-subtle put-down. In every place missionaries have ever gone, some form of belief system already existed. The missionaries show up and imply by their words and deeds that the existing native beliefs, rituals, and culture are faulty or misdirected. They say, "Convert and act as we better-informed, more- civilized foreigners, and you will be enlightened and saved." In other words, we are better than you; our prophets can beat up your prophets.

Perhaps in the case of head hunters or totally lawless societies, an argument could be made for a missionary benefit all the way around. But a Christian or Muslim trying to convert the other—what is the message? Organized religions should be above the level of Coke/Pepsi/Dr Pepper marketing wars. This argument seems superfluous, of course, if yours just happens to be the one, true, and exclusive way to believe and to experience God, and you see all other beliefs as bogus.

"Mine's better than yours" especially lives in the world of fundamentalism. They believe their scripture is the one and only, and absolutely true to the letter. The corollary is that all other faiths are wrong and perhaps evil. In the early days of religion, personal devotion and loyalty to the founding prophet was key. Once religion got organized, loyalty got organized too. Believers in any other message were labeled heretics, and eliminated if possible. This literal, exclusionist loyalty is now known as fundamentalism and is largely a Christian, Muslim, and to a lesser extent, Jewish phenomenon.

Each faith sees its group as the chosen people. All others are, of course, not chosen and are out of the club. The essence of fundamentalism in its many forms is to believe exactly as I believe and you're okay. Deviate from the one (my) true, exact belief in prescribed worship, and you are headed for hell.

Over the centuries, it has been easier and safer to believe as your parents and grandparents and fellow citizens believed than to actually figure out what you believe. If your neighborhood, church community, and society all reinforce family creed, who—other than the average teenager—can resist?

Take the case of young Pat Robason Jr., the only child of the Southern Senator, Senior Pat Robason. Paddy, as junior was called as a young post-bellum aristocrat, realized early on that he had a vocation. He didn't drink or smoke or dance—to avoid creating a damning record that might impede his entry into divinity school. He was known for his unusual sense of humor. Once in the eighth grade, so the story goes, he polished the school cannon of his military academy to rid it of the treasured brass patina. The school used the cannon as a testament to the antiquity and culture of the institution. But Pat thought the cannon should only be displayed in its original shining form, exactly as God made it. The joke was on Pat, however, because the cannon had actually been made by black slaves at a foundry in Virginia prior to the Civil War.

It is reported that Pat had a particular fondness for termites. Just as youngsters sometimes have pets, Pat kept a glass-enclosed termite farm. He watched fascinated as the termite colony built its nest from the raw materials of the earth. The construction process reminded him of spreading the faith—tearing down foreign, unorthodox structures and replacing them with the one, true, original design.

He did, in fact, graduate from the Most Self-Righteous College of Exclusive Truths during the 1950s and proceeded to spread the gospel according to Pat (formerly Paddy).

Fundamental, or heritage, holiness holds to strict and exact church canons and codes. The spirit of civil law takes a back seat to the letter of the religious law. The laws may differ by sect. But fundamentalism in whatever form follows the same pattern: strict observance of the immutable doctrines and rules. If it "says so" in the Bible, the Qur'an, the Book of Mormon, or whatever sacred text, it is the TRUTH forevermore.

Christianity, Judaism, and Islam, among other religions, all have a fundamentalist wing. Typically, these groups exhibit a highly literal and intolerant spirituality, and often campaign politically for hard-line social and moral policies. Christian fundamentalists forget Christ's compassion, just as Muslim fundamentalists forget the tolerance of the Qur'an, and Jewish fundamentalists the human rights of Arabs in the Holy Land. Believers worship the literal Bible or Qur'an and often are belligerently self-righteous.

American fundamentalism grew in reaction to Darwin's revolutionary assertion that all living things evolved, and therefore humans had not been placed on earth fully formed. The Bible and Qur'an had some explaining to do about Adam and Eve. Revivalist nineteenth century churches, and *The Fundamentals: A Testimony to the Truth* (a collection of seminal essays, published in 1917), went with "the Bible is right and Darwin is wrong."

Born-again (as though one infancy isn't enough) conversion is a dominant feature of American fundamentalism. The push for laws to prohibit teaching of evolution in public schools, central to the rise of the fundamentalist movement, climaxed with the 1925 Scopes Trial.

Fundamentalists frequently dislike the term *fundamentalism* and believe it should only apply to groups other than theirs. Many see the term as negative and anti-modern in the sense that it represents longing for a return to earlier times. They resist the fringe connotation and prefer to describe themselves as unwavering, orthodox, and true to the founder's original beliefs. They feel they alone have resisted the corruption of modern life, the corrosion of compromised beliefs, and the descent into modernism.

Literal interpretation of the Bible and the Qur'an lead fundamentalists to exclude and even denigrate believers of other creeds. The original Jewish concept of God was as just but not kind; tribal but not inclusive; harsh and retributive, not gentle or compassionate. This literal God is used by Christian fundamentalists as a rationale to reinforce their ideas of human shortcomings and prejudice. Onlookers often perceive this stance as "holier than thou" and accuse fundamentalists of confusing man-made doctrine and the ritual practice of religion with the essential moral, spiritual message of the holy founders. Mainstream believers say some fundamentalist movements are thinly disguised political causes wrapped in the shroud of religion and devotion.

Fundamentalists' strict and often passionate embrace of unchanging sacred truths has some interesting consequences in the world today. Unwavering devotion and belief can be valuable and pleasant, or be painful and cause great harm.

The Christian fundamentalist movement that believes the Old and New Testament Bible is historically complete, accurate, literal, and infallible has been growing in the United States. Certain cults believe a particular chosen individual is empowered to interpret the Bible. Generally the church is the interpreter, and the faithful believe they are not free to choose and are bound to follow the official church view.

Fundamentalism has also come to mean evangelical Christianity, or more precisely, evangelical Protestantism. Evangelicals tend to separate themselves from the main religious body by eschewing tobacco (opposite of what baseball players do); the modern evils of alcohol, music and dance; and especially modern translations of scriptures.

Most fundamentalism and evangelism is peaceful, ranging from benign to annoyingly persistent. But the late twentieth and early twenty-first centuries brought incessant news of violent and extreme religious fundamentalism.

Fundamentalists form two broad categories in the United States. The oldest and most dominant is the Billy Graham variety, known as revivalist, fundamentalist, evangelical Protestantism. Generally, this group stays out of politics and sticks to Crusade-scale, superbly organized, financially adept appeals to the forty percent of Americans who consider themselves evangelical. These folks believe God loves them and speaks to them.

After fifty years as the Pope of Protestant America, Graham presided over his last revival in June 2005. During the event, held in Flushing Meadows, NY, he entertained and preached to 240,000 people over three-plus days and, according to his website, 8,700 "committed their lives to Jesus Christ." True to form, he spoke of the Great Flood from the book of Genesis, the end of the world, and the need for the "saving power of the risen savior, Jesus Christ." His and the passion of the movement is saving your soul—with those literal instructions written in the Bible. This Madison Square Garden display of devotion attracted eighty Christian denominations and provided spiritual counseling in twenty languages. On-site and online financial contributions are encouraged: cash, check, PayPal, or money order.

The other brand of fundamentalism is the Jerry Falwell (RIP)/Pat Robertson/Ralph Reed type. They readily mixed and promoted the two subjects our moms cautioned us to avoid in polite conversation: religion and politics. The Christian Coalition is the father (not mother) organization of much of the Christian right wing. Their website lists them as a "political organization," but does not show an annual report or financial statements, presumably because they are chartered as a church or religious entity.

Their political agenda includes balanced budgets, lower taxes, choice in education, term limits, and political reform. They support anti- abortion, anti-euthanasia, and anti-homosexual issues: the pro-family policy.

Intelligent design is the counter-science modern movement to reinstate the Bible into biology and genetics. The concept promotes the biblical view as an alternate to the theory of evolution. Proponents of intelligent design claim there is no more proof for the ideas of Darwin than for those of the Bible. They want their theological theory taught alongside the scientific theory of evolution. Opponents say, "Believe what you want, but don't confuse intelligent design with scientific method."

A parallel in the Roman Catholic world is traditional Catholicism, which repudiates the reforms of the Second Vatican Council (1962–1965) as mere pastoral advice. Some fundamentalist Catholics hold Vatican II to be mistaken. They feel these Council changes can be discounted or ignored without compromising their faith, and disavow attempts at reconciliation with other separated Christians. They favor the Latin Mass and object to the creeping influence of modern life and recent changes to traditional Church rituals and practices. Like other fundamentalists, they consider theirs the true faith, and the main body of Catholic religion too lax or in error. Pope Benedict XVI seemed to be of this school.

Islamic fundamentalism similarly subscribes to the concept of literal interpretation of the Qur'an and strict adherence to its rules and laws. They oppose liberal Islam that makes concessions to modernity. Muslim conservatives abhor that liberals accept conceptual interpretations of the Qur'an and tolerate other beliefs.

More radical than Muslim fundamentalists, Islamists don't believe in a secular or political state at all. Islamists advocate a state governed exclusively and absolutely by Islamic law. Ayatollahs, for example, rule Iran with a puppet civil government. The Taliban, prior to their ouster, similarly controlled Afghanistan.

In Judaism, fundamentalism can be found in certain Orthodox sects. For some Buddhists, fundamentalism takes the form of believing their school is true and those from other schools are heretics. Although Hinduism is generally known for its tolerance, some have claimed the nationalistic Hindutva movement has fundamentalist tendencies.

Belief in the inerrancy of the supposedly original and fundamental sacred texts creates an attitude among fundamentalists. Their self-appointed group is absolutely right on matters of faith and doctrine. "God is on our side" is the call sign. They loathe the creeping influence of secular, modern society on the purported original and pristine beliefs of their founders. Frequently they deny the rights of women and homosexuals. They often emphasize the inherent weakness and fallibility of humans. They see redemption only by their particular brand of "fundamental" grace. Few of them will read this book.

What are children and young adults to think when exposed to their elders' hate and discrimination? They've been taught to follow "one way," to consider other points of view misguided and evil, and to try to force the conversion of others. They truly believe theirs is the only valid religion and their God is better than your God. Breaking the mold and thinking outside the bias box become unlikely.

Some argue that the cure for fundamentalism should involve diminishing religion and encouraging a secular society. But secular groups such as the Anti-Defamation League, Americans United for the Separation of Church and State, and the ACLU can go overboard in their protests. They argue against even the mention of God or religion in political discourse. They may go so far as to discard morality as they guard the separation of church from state. Author/preacher Jim Wallis believes better religion, not secularism, is the antidote for fundamentalism.

Better religion, however, is easier said than done. When Christianity turned corporate and was backed by the Roman Empire, dissension was outlawed. Heretics became crispy critters on a stick. Today, the threat of spiritual toasting in hell works as an emotional threat against independent thinkers. Dissension may lead to family friction and social ostracism as well as cancellation of your parish newsletter or televangelism subscription.

Islam struggles, too, with minority fundamentalists who insist on literal interpretations of religious doctrine. Dissent and modern interpretation to them are heresy and/or apostasy and punishable by physical harm or death. Car bomb incineration has replaced burning at the stake, with amazingly similar results: death to the individuals, but seldom permanent social change.

In this scientific and fact-based world, fundamentalist Christians and Muslims find it increasingly difficult to argue a literal Adam and Eve in the Bible or Qur'an. Likewise it's hard to scientifically defend a historical Noah and actual worldwide flood. In their attempt to make a literal case, they destroy the credibility of the important underlying message of duty to God or Allah and to our fellow human beings.

Many groups believe their God is best. In a way ironically they're correct—in the sense that the God of each group is one and the same. But for some radical members of each belief system this is not answer enough. They'll fight to proclaim the exclusivity of their proprietary God and to discredit others' beliefs.

# RELIGIOUS ZEALOTS, FANATICS, AND TERRORISTS

*Absolute faith corrupts absolutely.* —*Eric Hoffer*

Zealot comes from Hebrew and means someone jealous for God in the literal and fundamentalist sense. The term originated with the first century Jewish group that advocated violence and forbade compromise with the Romans. They fought and subverted the peace process, fomenting revolt and sabotage in the quest for fundamentalist orthodoxy in Judaism. They even killed their own kinsmen—those they thought were collaborators with the enemy. The Zealots represented a violent escalation of "my religion is better than yours." They demonstrated the extreme bias of religious passion gone awry. "Believe as we believe or die," they said as they delivered death and destruction to others and ultimately themselves.

The Romans finally responded with the destruction of the Temple in Jerusalem, killing many Jews and dispersing and enslaving the rest. The Jewish Talmud specifically condemns the Zealots for their aggression and unwillingness to compromise and thereby save Jewish lives and the Temple.

Religious history is littered with the bodies of the not-faithful- enough. The legendary Judas, perhaps a Zealot, may have turned traitor to Jesus because he thought Jesus a not-orthodox-enough Jew.

Zealots and terrorists have persecuted Jews, Christians, Muslims, Buddhists, Hindus, Sikhs, Baha'is, Mormons, and most historical faiths. As a common theme, these perpetrators believe they act according to the will of God. They believe they defend the original, true, and faithful religion. They are fundamentalists gone wild.

Digging a little deeper, Jessica Stern, in *Terror in the Name of God*, says terrorists' testimonials often mask "fear of a godless universe, of chaos, of loose rules, and of loneliness—fears that we all have to one degree or another." In an interview prior to publication of her book, she observed that terrorists are initially attracted to the idea of following the will of God. "Over time, the leaders recruit youth into seeing the world in that way. I think some of them become quite cynical. They become professional killers."

American social writer Eric Hoffer thinks fanatics were not so much just or holy as desperate for something to hold onto, and ruthless in their dedication to a holy cause.

Excessive or psychotic enthusiasm for preserving, or for reforming and changing, the religious status quo have wreaked havoc on society over the ages. Whether to support tribe, country, or religion, killing aggression has been used in the name of fanatical devotion.

Dozens of terrorist groups have been active in Iraq, Israel, Palestine, and more recently in the United States, Great Britain, and Spain. All have seen violence in the name of religion tied to politics. Islamic groups have been most active recently, but Christian groups also have left scars. The nominally Christian Ku Klux Klan terrorized blacks in America in the name of religion. Catholics and Protestants terrorized each other and bystanders in Ireland.

These terrorist holders of the Truth kill wantonly, while believing they are making the world secure for their brand of religion.

The suicide bomber has upped the destructive ante. Extremist Muslims, encouraged by radical Muslim clerics, believe suicide an acceptable and even a devout religious act. Moderates believe suicide to be a perversion of the Qur'an and an immoral practice not consistent with Islam. But the ideal of ultimate sacrifice has been gaining traction, particularly among the young and disaffected. They believe that by killing infidels and acting in horrific ways to evangelize the cause of Islam, they earn a place in paradise. Unfortunately and ironically, the Crusaders heading off to convert and/or kill Muslim infidels also thought they earned a plenary indulgence and their place in heaven.

The primary difference setting today's terrorism apart from earlier brands is wholesale targeting of civilians. They make for easier prey than military and political victims. This tactic usually fails. Persecution and terrorism have the opposite of their intended effect. If we look at history, we see that persecuted Christians flourished, as did Muslims and others. Yet the carnage goes on. The pull of the gang, the influence of peers, and the macho belief that "might makes right" may long be with us—especially when salted by religious fervor.

Separating religious from political motivations is a dicey proposition. The U.S.-Iraq war may have been about freeing an oppressed religious majority from a ruthless dictator and/or about ensuring a secure supply of oil. The enemy Sunni insurgents might have been fighting for orthodox Islam and/or they might have been interested in regaining their oppressive minority political power. Much evil and good have been done in the name of God, yet secretly in the cause of evil. Not to discount noble intentions, but human nature usually finds a rationale for human actions, whether they be good or bad.

United States attention focused sharply on extremist Muslim terrorism after the destruction of the World Trade Center on September 11, 2001. The 9/11 Commission reports, "This immeasurable pain [of the attack] was inflicted by 19 young Arabs acting at the behest of Islamist extremists headquartered in distant Afghanistan." The report goes on to summarize numerous attacks from 1993 and describes a 1998 *fatwa* [Islamic decree] issued by Osama bin Laden, leader of al Qaeda, and others, declaring it was God's decree that every Muslim try his utmost to kill any American, military or civilian, anywhere in the world, because of American occupation of Islam's holy places and aggression against Muslims.

The report stated, "The enemy is not just 'terrorism.' It is the threat posed specifically by Islamist terrorism, by bin Laden and others who draw on a long tradition of extreme intolerance within a minority strain of Islam that does not distinguish politics from religion, and distorts both. The enemy is not Islam, the great world faith, but a perversion of Islam."

Extremist Muslims care little about commission reports or other political or religious points of view. The key question is how moderate Muslims will control and eliminate those who abuse and distort the practice of Islam.

"What possessed you to attempt suicide?" asked Nasra Hassan, a Pakistani Muslim, in the November 2001 *New Yorker* article summarized by freemuslim.org. She compiled information about more than two hundred Muslim suicide bombers and tells of a Palestinian man she calls S, who survived a failed suicide attack on an Israeli bus. Five years later, S—now a local Gaza wounded hero whom "Allah 'brought back to life'"—told

Hassan what possessed him. He said the detonator on his body bomb was the key to Paradise and that the journey to kill was a joyful trip to martyrdom. He and his deeply religious comrades, he said, swore on the Qur'an to their Hamas planner not to waver in their quest for military and spiritual glory.

Along with spiritual glory come other benefits: three to five thousand US dollars to the bomber's family, the instant washing away of his sins, seventy-two beautiful virgins in paradise, and a free pass for seventy of his nearest relatives on the Day of Resurrection. A member of Hamas explained the suicide attacker's preparation as a focus on achieving the presence of Allah and Muhammad, and on fighting the Israeli occupation.

The lead-up to the suicide operation is described as intensely spiritual, including two to four hours of daily lectures, as well as prayers and fasting. Video documentation is shown to pump up the attacker and is used for future recruitment. "He puts a Koran in his left breast pocket, above the heart, he straps [on] the explosives," according to Hassan, and he heads off for the attack. As he presses the detonator to blow up his victims and himself, he says, "Allahu akbar"—"Allah is great. All praise to Him."

Because suicide is forbidden in the Qur'an, these operations are euphemistically called *sacred explosions.*

Reportedly, the Tamil Tigers, a militant group of Sri Lanka terrorists, invented the explosive vest and used it to kill Rajiv Gandhi in a 1991 suicide attack. The BBC reported in May 2000 that the Tigers executed more than five times as many suicide attacks as all other groups combined. Although the Tigers use terrorism and suicide, they do not have a strong religious basis. Some say they have a Marxist orientation. Their main cause is fighting for a separate territory in northeastern Sri Lanka, a country in which the political division is primarily between Hindus and Buddhists.

Many terrorist groups and individuals throughout history expected to die, or at least knew they were facing very long odds of survival. In the old days, a terrorist typically had to get close to a well-guarded target, make the kill, and attempt an unlikely escape. The risk was high, but with some hope of survival. The now-infamous bomb vest—or backpack or shoes—is nearly impossible to defend against, and therefore makes for a very effective killing device. But it comes with "no deposit, no return"— and no possibility for a refund. The terrorist knows there is no chance of surviving a successful attack.

Robert Pape, professor of political science at the University of Chicago, completed a database of every suicide terrorist attack from 1980 to 2004 and concluded Islamic fundamentalism is not as closely associated with suicide terrorism as people think. Interestingly, his book *Dying to Win: The Strategic Logic of Suicide Terrorism* is reviewed and touted on the websites of The American Conservative (Pat Buchanan, isolationist) as well as BuzzFlash (liberal, anti-Bush, anti-GOP). This may speak to the independent nature of Pape's work, or maybe to the widespread opposition to the Iraq war.

According to Pape, in an *American Conservative* interview (July 2005), the common element in the suicide attacks is defense of their homeland from military occupying forces. Pape claims "every major suicide-terrorist campaign…has had as its central objective to compel a democratic state to withdraw." Religion matters when the occupying force has different religious beliefs from those of the occupied. He says that provides the opportunity for the terrorist leaders to "demonize the occupier in especially vicious ways." Pape notes that Islam is not the only religious group to recruit suicide terrorists. He points to the attacks in Lebanon in the 1980s, in which eight attackers were Islamic, twenty-seven were Communists and socialists, and three were Christians.

Fundamentalist beliefs melded with political agendas have supported many extremist travesties. Certainly, in the Middle Ages, the Crusades and Muslim conquests had major political elements. Some suggest that, then and now, fundamentalism is merely or primarily a political recruiting tool. But the doctrine and the acts of violence seem joined at the hip. Perhaps it doesn't matter whether the doctrine is political or religious. What matters is the violence to others, particularly to innocent civilians who may not even know about the ideology of the terrorist. Some even say suicide bombers, their instigators, and other terrorists really care about control of real estate and merely use religious fanaticism as a tool.

The terrorist typically rationalizes, premeditates, and plans his or her attack. Often, he or she is educated and not impoverished. The subway bombings in London in 2005 present an interesting question: What motivated these middle-class—half with college training—young men to perpetrate such indiscriminate acts of violence? Many terrorists are said to be weak in their religious knowledge and beliefs, and therefore susceptible to undue influence by manipulative religious leaders. Maybe it's an unfortunate mix of fundamentalist training, a convincing political rationale (such as defending the homeland or creating a utopia), and their weak character that leads to the willingness to commit any crime. Maybe they have a macho need to make a powerful statement to demonstrate a perverted sort of heroism. The frustration of youthful impatience and the inability to overcome the inertia of a slow and orderly civil process may lead them to the instant final solution of terrorist suicide.

Dr. Daniel Pipes, a controversial anti-Islamist, asks, "If militant Islam is the problem and moderate Islam is the solution... how does one differentiate between these two forms of Islam?" In "Finding Moderate Muslims," an article in the November 26, 2003 issue of *Jerusalem Post*, Pipes lists a set of differentiating questions, which are summarized here according to the categories given by Pipes:

- Violence: Do you support terrorism and terrorist organizations?
- Modernity: Do you accept other religions and the rights of women?
- Secularism: Do you support equal civil rights for all and respect for non-Muslim majority government?
- Islamic pluralism: Are Shi'ites fully legitimate Muslims and are former believers not condemned?
- Self-criticism: Is spiritual and academic study and inquiry of the Qur'an acceptable?
- Self-defense: Do you accept enhanced security to fight militant Islam?
- Goals in the West: Will you seek to transform Christian countries into Muslim ones ruled by Islamic law?"

Pipes believes "these questions offer a good start to the vexing issue of separating enemy from friend."

The questions were answered by the key al Qaeda operative in Iraq, the late Abu Musab al-Zarqawi. He repeatedly called for death to the disbelievers and anyone standing nearby.

At a conference titled "A World Without Zionism," Iranian President Ahmadinejad personified the zealot approach: "We are in the process of a historical war between the World of Arrogance [the West] and the Islamic world.... Is it possible for us to witness a world without America and

Zionism? You had best know that this slogan and this goal is attainable, and surely can be achieved." Ahmadinejad's chief strategist, Hassan Abbasi, amplified: "We have a strategy drawn up for the destruction of Anglo-Saxon civilization." Moderates in Iran have their work cut out for them.

Saudi Arabia also has much to overcome. Alex Alexiev, in the November 2005 *National Review*, believes there are two key issues we Westerners refuse to accept. The first is that "Islamism does not concern religion, but rather sedition and incitement to violence and murder." He adds that the second issue is that this violence and murder "[are] almost always state sponsored." He says the Islamofascists are out to destroy our "liberal civilization and its norms of freedom, democracy, secularism and human rights." He lays much of the blame on our so-called allies Saudi Arabia and Pakistan. He says Saudi Arabia admits to spending an average of $2.5 billion per year for the past three decades to support Islamic activities, including building and controlling "210 Islamic centers, 1,500 mosques, 2,000 schools, and 200 colleges in non-Muslim countries alone. As a result, there is hardly a Western city today that does not have an Islamist-controlled institution… spewing hatred against the West and Muslims who refuse to submit to radical [fundamentalist] Islam." Much more potent than al Qaeda, this "infrastructure of extremist mosques, madrasas, 'charities,' and foundations… [is] the real incubator of fanaticism worldwide."

Mark Twain's early-1900s take on organized religions:

> Man is the religious animal. He is the only religious animal. He is the only animal that has the True Religion—several of them. He is the only animal that loves his neighbor as himself and cuts his throat, if his theology isn't straight. He has made a graveyard of the globe in trying his honest best to smooth his brother's path to happiness and heaven.

Twain was commenting on the human tendency to value religion, especially our own brand of religion, above all else, and to impose it on others.

Radical Islamists who spew religious hate and intolerance, however, are having more than a little trouble these days targeting only their preferred audiences. Playing just to their constituents or their congregations is becoming nearly impossible because translation services (MEMRI) and the press generally are watching and listening, and reporting in the media and especially on the Internet.

As Thomas Friedman in a July 22, 2005 editorial in The New York Times puts it, "You [extremists] are free to say what you want, but we are free to listen, to let the whole world know what you are saying and to protect every free society from hate spreaders like you."

We've seen how humans have always paid homage to someone or something. Fear, awe, belonging to the tribe, survival, security—all are understandable reasons to gather in the community of religion. Religious societies have always sought to be exclusive, beginning with new and larger tribes excluding members of other tribes. "My God is better than your God" is as ancient as human development. History is filled with preferred gods falling out of fashion and being replaced by new beliefs. The favored king or queen and his or her favorite god were continually replaced by a new king or queen with yet a newer favorite belief.

Since Adamino and before, somebody has always been ready to provide (and substitute) an interpretation of the holy and spiritual. This made sense for centuries because few were educated and the options for spiritual choices were limited. Quantum change came with widespread education, triggered first by the printing press and now by the Internet.

Organized religions coalesced around spiritual entrepreneurs whom we call prophets. Organizers followed the prophet and built institutions, even if that was not the prophet's intent at all. Bureaucracies then blossomed and defenders of bureaucracies and of the status quo followed them. Bevies of bureaucrats beget dozens of dogmas. Catholics argue that God as a three-in-one Trinity is important, but would Jesus have agreed? Christians generally insist on the Virgin birth: what would Jesus say about that? Muslims argue for universal Islam: would Muhammad have countered with respect for other Peoples of the Book? Thus, what typically began as a prophet's protest to religious abuses, became, in turn, new religious abuses, frequently at odds with the original message.

Not a flattering description, of course, and devoid of the centuries of solace and inspiration provided by religion to millions of people, but real in a bottom-line sort of way. The world religions have much in common: a holy founder who challenged the status quo; followers; devotees; defenders; and fanatic defenders—in some cases, violent, fanatic, zealot defenders.

Ironically, zealots credit themselves with the survival of religion itself. Any deviation from the supposed literal message they see as an attack on the faith itself. They see themselves as the guardians of religious truth and purity. In reality, zealots give religion a bad name. No founder of a major religion would condone the death and destruction zealous terrorists visit on innocent people. Jesus would condemn the Crusades, and Muhammad the car bombings in crowded market places. Nothing about their teachings suggest otherwise.

But don't take my word for it. Let's look together at the important elements of the major existing, traditional world religions. How can we know what to believe ourselves if we don't know the basics of each religion? How can we even hazard a guess as to "what Jesus *would* say?"

Thousands of books have been written about each faith. I have pulled together brief summaries, listing those general elements with which most would agree. Please use this is a starting point. Go out and find more information about anything that piques your interest. I think you'll find it is important for your spiritual choices today to know how religions evolved, to have a picture of how the messages warped over time. Knowing what others believe can be of great help in understanding where we are now as a nation and as a world-people, and what personal spiritual choices are yours to make.

# SECTION THREE

# A QUICK SUMMARY
# OF WORLD RELIGIONS

# JUDAISM

*It's more the good deeds than the creeds.*

Judaism believes in and honors God as a Supreme Being. Jews are instructed by the Torah, or Hebrew Bible, to live a moral and perfecting life in this world, to revere parents and teachers, to support the community, and to engage in acts of loving kindness.

Abraham was the first of the great prophets of Judaism. He is thought to have lived about 2000 BCE, and according to Jewish tradition was descended from Adam, Adamino, and Noah.

Abraham was the patriarch of the Jews through his son Isaac. In the Old Testament, Abraham's willingness to sacrifice his son Isaac demonstrated his faith and obedience to God. Because of his act of faith (child abuse under current laws), God promised Abraham's heirs would be the "chosen people." Chosen people (as well as "older is better") have always been popular features of organized religions.

Moses lived about 1400 BCE and was acclaimed the prophet of God, or Yahweh, as God was called back then. In exile from Egypt, Moses encountered Yahweh at the energy-efficient burning bush, where God revealed His name and Moses agreed to lead the enslaved Hebrews from Egypt. We all "know" the Jews crossed the parted Red Sea. More likely it was the Sea of Reeds—endangered wetlands—and they had to step on some endangered species as they went. Good trick, Moses; it was tough terrain for the Egyptian chariots and horse riders, who surely got bogged down in the muck.

Christians also consider Moses a great prophet, and Muslims highly regard him as the prophet of the Jews and the recipient of scripture and the law.

Moses and probably some later buddies wrote the Torah, which began as the Pentateuch, the first five books. The Torah morphed over time to encompass all of Jewish religious knowledge, rituals, and laws. *Torah* literally means "instruction" or "teaching."

Judaism is one of the oldest of the world's great religions. Supposedly begun in Israel some four thousand years ago, it barely makes it as a major religion today, with only about fifteen million followers around the world (six million Jews perished in the Holocaust). Most Jewish people live in Israel or the United States. France hosts the largest Jewish group in Europe.

Judaism is not so much about theology, dogma, and creeds, as it is about the values of daily living. It is a way-of-life religion. Jews promise God to live by His principles, not just for their own sakes, but for the betterment of the whole world. Judaism does not seek converts. Those who convert to Judaism must undertake the observance of the Torah (a serious commitment for uncircumcised gentile males).

The Torah and the Talmud (a record of Jewish oral law and tradition) are held as the word of God. Jews see studying the Torah and Talmud as necessary to getting close to God. For Jews, God is personal. As a result, they may have individual interpretations that are not necessarily enforced by the establishment.

Jews un-sacrilegiously believe humans are made in the image of God and should be as God-like as possible in life. They believe obeying the law means doing God's will and showing respect and love for God. Observers sometimes joke that Christians "keep the faith" and Jews "keep the commandments." Judaism is action-oriented more than faith-based: Jews believe their actions here and now determine their fate both on earth and in the hereafter. However, what happens HERE is more central than what happens in the hereafter.

Like clergy to religion, Jews are bonded to Israel, the milk-and- honey land God promised to Abraham, and in particular to the holy city of Jerusalem. As Jeremiah prophesized in 600 BCE, the original temple in Jerusalem (built by King Solomon in 950 BCE) was destroyed, and the Jews forced into exile, after they revolted against the Babylonians. Jeremiah, among greatest of the many prophets, apparently wrote or at least collected the works of the Old Testament. He remains well respected today in the Jewish community.

The Jewish scholar Hillel, who lived from about 70 BCE to 10 CE, was asked to summarize the essence of Judaism. He reportedly responded: "What is hateful to you, do not do to your neighbor: this is the whole of Jewish law; the rest is mere commentary." Pithy chap.

Like virtually all organized religions, Judaism has taken disparate paths. Here are summaries of the four main forms of Judaism today.

**Orthodox Judaism**, or traditional Judaism, views the Hebrew Bible in a literalist, fundamentalist way, and ignores modern biblical scholarly study and commentary not supporting that view. Orthodox Jews see exact study and practice of the Torah as ideal human existence. They believe all is divinely ordained—as in "no grain of sand on any beach moves without God's permission."

**Reform Judaism** originated when European Jews began to live outside ghettos and to blend with other groups. It holds to the notion of progressive revelation; that is, each generation can redefine and expand upon the principles of faith. Early reforms saw personal ethics as more central than rituals to their definition of Judaism. However, more recent reforms have reinstituted some of the traditional rituals.

**Conservative Judaism** began as a reaction to the Jewish reformers and their turning away from tradition. It currently holds the largest group of American Jews and orbits the New York Jewish Theological Seminary. They advocate slow and measured changes not too disturbing to the practice of Jewish faith. Conservative liturgy and worship represent a middle way between Orthodox and Reform, with a mix of Hebrew and English at different temples.

**Reconstructionist Judaism** is based substantially on the work of a Conservative rabbi, Mordecai Kaplan, *Judaism as a Civilization* (1934). It recasts Judaism in a modern scientific way and defines the "God-idea" as an ever-developing human awareness and experience.

Like all religions, Judaism has evolved over the centuries. Looking at some passages in the Torah, it is clear that we look at things differently today, and literal interpretations of ancient scriptures may cause some heartburn. For example, "You shall utterly destroy them [the Canaanite nations that refuse to leave Israel]... as the Lord your God commanded you..." (Deuteronomy 20:17-18) And "Joshua... Moses' successor, undertakes to subjugate and destroy these surrounding and hostile groups." Likewise, "an eye for an eye" ("life for a life" Exodus 21:23 – 21:25) sounds like severe retributive justice, but Rabbi Telushkin, in *Jewish Literacy,* says it actually softens an earlier harsher law. Prior to this reform, revenge greater than the original harm was a distinct possibility.

Justice is a big part of Judaism. In the words of Telushkin, "performing deeds of justice is perhaps the most important obligation Judaism imposes on the Jew." In the old days this meant giving ten percent of your income to the poor. Today it mostly means cheerfully giving what you can afford.

According to Telushkin, all who believe in one God and practice moral behavior are "ethical monotheists, and thus natural allies of religiously committed Jews."

Judaism, then, in its most essential form, believes in and honors God as a Supreme Being. Jews are instructed by the Torah to revere their parents and teachers, to support the community and to engage in acts of loving kindness, all in the here and now.

# HINDUISM

*The essence of every soul is eternal.*

Hinduism believes humans are a little bit of heaven—that is, all part of God. Our job is to live our daily lives through *dharma* (law and duties), to act and meditate our way toward our divine nature, and to liberate ourselves from the cycle of life and death so we can attain nirvana.

Hinduism dates to the second millennium BCE and is likely the second-oldest major modern world religion and philosophy. It really doesn't have a Moses, Muhammad, or Jesus as a single founding prophet. Rather, its development can be traced back through its scriptural tradition. The earliest Hindu scriptures are the Vedas—oral revelations, hymns, and ritual texts that were written down by the ancient sages around 1500 BCE. These teach of infinite manifestations of God and describe how dharma should be lived.

Vedic philosophy is distilled in the Upanishads (800 to 400 BCE), texts that describe how one can realize through contemplation and meditation that the soul (atman) is united with the Ultimate Truth (Brahman, or God). They also tell us about *karma*—good things happen to good people (and you know the rest).

Another text dating from around that time is the *Mahabharata*, one of the longest epics ever written, replete with a cast of thousands and plenty of soap-opera drama. Its most famous section is the *Bhagavad Gita* (its title translates as "Divine Song"), which over the centuries came to serve as a Hindu bible. The *Bhagavad Gita* took earlier Hindu ritual sacrifice and impersonal, priestly knowledge and combined them with personal worship to delineate the path of karma yoga. Comparing your life with the warrior Arjuna—listening to his guru, Lord Krishna, convince him why he must enter the battlefield and fight, even if it means killing his dear friends and family—who wouldn't breathe a sigh of relief and add a little meditation and devotion to insure things go well in this life and the next?

The Puranic scriptures appeared in the time of the Gupta Empire (320 to 540 CE) and contain narratives of the history of the universe, from creation to destruction, including genealogies of kings, heroes, and demigods, and descriptions of Hindu cosmology and geography. The Guptas identified themselves as the human representatives of Vishnu, at that time the main deity, and endowed the construction of stone temples. (Even then politicians loved ribbon cuttings and enduring monuments.)

Beginning in the thirteenth century and by the seventeenth century, India was largely controlled by the invading Mogul empire. Some Hindus converted to Islam and others remained Hindu but adopted some Muslim beliefs and practices. Poet-saint Kabir (1440–1518), born a Muslim, became a devotee of Lord Rama and disciple of the Hindu guru Ramananda.

Kabir believed we are all children of one God, be He called Rama or Allah. His own life taught him that people should not be separated by labels of social caste or bound and tied by the ropes of religious dogma. He saw no use for external worship, either Hindu or Muslim. Instead he sounded a call for worship of the one true God within each being. That God, whom he liked to address as the "Secret One," was nothing but pure love. He said,

> Friend, if you've never really met the Secret One, what is the
> source of your self-confidence?
> Stop all this flirtation using words.
> Love does not happen with words.
> Don't lie to yourself about the holy books and what they say.
> The love I talk of is not in the books.
> Who has wanted it has it.

Kabir re-emphasized the Hindu tradition that each believer needs a spiritual guide in the form of a guru. Charismatic gurus followed in his footsteps, creating a blending of Hindu and Muslim thought. The Sikh religion was founded by a Kabir disciple, Nanak (1469–1539), who attacked distinctions of caste and the worship of images, while keeping many of the personal and family religious rituals that were at the heart of

Hindu piety. Sikhs eventually became a distinct religious group, having been rejected by both Hindus and Muslims.

Hinduism was strongly influenced by Ram Mohan Roy (1772– 1833), who attempted to reconcile it with the modern social and scientific advancements and discoveries of the eighteenth and nineteenth centuries. It continues to evolve and diversify in the twenty-first century.

What is contemporary Hinduism? It is nearly naked holy men traipsing about Hindu temples and pilgrims by the millions taking a soul-scrubbing dip in the Ganges. It is also the Western businessman or woman performing private *puja* (honor or worship) at home every morning before going to the office. It is the yoga class, offered at your local rec center, that's good for your waistline as well as your psyche. Everything from life-cycle rites to bloody goat sacrifices to the silent sacrifice of a meditative yogi fall under the umbrella of contemporary Hindu practice.

Nearly nine hundred million people identify as Hindus and inhabit primarily India, Nepal, and Bangladesh, making it the third largest world religion. Hinduism is unlike Christianity and other Western religions. Christians often treat their religion as a particular part of life—think Sunday Mass—and only remotely associate it with business or social or political life. (Christian until out of the church parking lot.) Hindus characteristically integrate religion into their daily social and work lives. They aren't big on community or congregational worship, but do have temples that draw many thousands of Indians pilgrims. (The Indian temple best know to Westerners, the Taj Mahal, is a mausoleum built by a Muslim ruler.) Most Hindus, though, worship privately or with their families at home shrines.

Many would describe Hinduism as a moral/ethical philosophy or way of life. It doesn't hold to a single central doctrine, but rather includes a wide range of beliefs and practices. There is no Pope with a final say in matters of faith or even ritual. Most Hindus, however, believe in a single divinity or Supreme God, Brahman, who is present in all things. Most, additionally, believe in other gods who are aspects or manifestations of that Supreme God. For example, some sects uphold the so-called Hindu Trinity, consisting of Brahma (who creates), Vishnu (who sustains), and Shiva (who consumes) everything in the universe.

Virtually all Hindus believe in *samsara*—the birth, death, and rebirth cycle of the human soul. Belief in karma is nearly universal and perhaps the tenet most widely known in the West. Karma says "what goes around, comes around," or good actions cause good effects. And vice versa. In other words, the quality of our life HERE and now and in the future depends on our behavior in the past.

Historically, Hinduism has not been evangelical; its members have not tried to convert people. But some Hindu groups today do actively seek new members. They do not do it in an evangelical manner, like in Christianity or Islam, however. There is no ritual for conversion, and you don't have to give up your old beliefs, as in most conversions. You can be Hindu and still believe in the Christian or Muslim God.

Hinduism evolves as people today add their personal bits of wisdom, knowledge, and experience to the collected beliefs of the religion. You might describe it as Wiki-religious (like the online, anyone-edit encyclopedia) or like an open-source computer programming language such as Linux, in which everybody contributes and the results remain in common human ownership. No one really has the last word. In fact, Hinduism holds there cannot be a single interpretation, so it is difficult to generalize.

The lack of a founder (and the application period for that appears to have closed) does not seem to have had a negative impact on its survival as a creed.

Some Hindus today are concerned about the vanilla-ization of the many Hindu sects and denominations. To complement their tolerance for other faiths, Hindu leaders argue for universal diversity. But they object to encroachment and proselytizing by other religions in India and areas predominantly Hindu. According to the April 15, 2005 *National Catholic Reporter,* Pope John Paul II visited India in November of 1999 and declared, "Just as the first millennium saw the cross firmly planted in the soil of Europe and the second in that of America and Africa, so may the third Christian millennium witness a great harvest of faith on this vast and vital continent." Who, we might ask, invited him?

This polarization of religion has been accentuated by the ending of the caste system. Officially, it was abolished in 1949. However, it remains a serious and sometimes embarrassing problem. Discrimination is particularly hard on *Dalits*—those who were traditionally considered untouchables by the other four castes. Assistance (read affirmative action) from the Indian government has helped, especially in urban areas.

Some Dalits have taken the matter into their own hands and abandoned Hinduism. Many have converted to Buddhism and others to Christianity. The backlash in some circles has been anger toward religions seeking converts from the Hindu faith.

Nevertheless, in its essence, Hinduism holds and accepts many diverse beliefs and is tolerant of other religions. Hindus typically believe in an eternal spirit, and that all humans and all things are part of God. Their main life task is to realize their potential through daily actions, and to seek and find their divine nature within (the HERE), thus earning liberation from the cycle of life and death (by coming to know they are one with that which transcends both the here and the hereafter).

# CHINESE TRADITIONAL RELIGIONS

*Respect your elders and be true to human nature in yourself and others.*

Confucianism and Taoism (along with Buddhism, treated separately here) are frequently lumped together with various "folk" religions and called Chinese Traditional Religions. Many variations in beliefs, rituals, and practice exist, but collectively the two may claim a total of four hundred million practitioners worldwide, making them the fourth largest religious group.

Confucianism embraces the learning of human history and follows the principles of ethical and righteous behavior, whether you are a king or gentleman, or if you are in politics. It generally believes in the goodness and perfectibility of humans and their social institutions, and calls for special respect for parents and the elders (some suspect ancient editing by parents and elders).

Confucius, the founder of Confucianism, is also known as K'ung Fu-tzu, or The Great Master K'ung. Born in China in 551 BCE, he died in 479 (both plus or minus some years). He became the founder of a major world religion/philosophy practiced primarily in China, Korea, Vietnam, and Japan. Born of a low-ranking noble family that struggled to provide the basic necessities, Confucius apparently educated himself. He became a high official in his local province, only to grow disenchanted with politics (imagine that!) and leave to initiate his own social reforms.

He wandered and preached throughout the local regions during a time of constant feuds at the end of the feudal era. He returned to his home state of Lu (now Shandong, southeast of Beijing), having gathered some three thousand followers. He taught that the solution to the internecine warfare of his day was a return to the virtuous traditions of the enlightened emperors of antiquity, especially those of the Chou dynasty, from 1000 to about 250 BCE.

Confucius preached a type of humanism, meaning you should be true to your nature and (in a Jesus preview) not do to others what you would not have them do to you. One of his disciples summed things up by saying, "The doctrine of our master is to be true to the principles of our nature and the benevolent exercise of them to others—this and nothing more." (Sound familiar?) Confucius downplayed the merely practical in favor of virtue as an end in itself. He appealed to the logical mind as a means to ultimately reach a type of heaven characterized by peace and harmony. Like parents of all ages, he detested the popular music (BCE Rap?) and rites of his day as lacking virtue and harmony. He sought a return to more traditional music (golden oldies).

Confucius focused on the gentleman (or woman?) of character, rather than nobility, and encouraged his followers to practice virtue for its own sake. He emphasized life in the present moment, but talked of heaven as a manifestation of the virtuous life. To him, however, heaven and earth were not seen as fundamentally separate, but rather as a joining of the HERE and the hereafter. Although some attempts were made to deify Confucius, he escaped being put on such a high pedestal and retained his reputation as a wise but human teacher and is still regarded as a prophet today.

Four Confucian perspectives emerged following Confucius' death: Mencius, stressing the inherent goodness of man; The Doctrine of Man, similarly emphasizing the metaphysical and sincere (heavenly) nature of man; The Great Learning, promoting maximum learning as a way to bring world peace; and Hsun Tzu, declaring that human nature was evil and needed laws and rules, but arguing people could overcome their evil nature through the process of learning. Initially, Hsun Tzu won out, and around 200 BCE formed a school under the Han dynasty. It evolved into a prep course for government service as well as a study of Confucian classic thought.

A kind of social engineering/social restructuring evolved around the year 1000, but failed long term. This (Neo-)Confucianism, influenced by the introduction of Buddhist thought, revived first the emphasis on family values, and later became an individual ethical discipline.

Confucianism prevailed as the state orthodoxy from 200 BCE all the way to the early twentieth century, when being a Confucianist no longer bought entry to government service. By about 1930, it was no longer the official state religion. In spite of repression by the Communists, however,

Confucianism continues as an important personal ethical belief and philosophy in much of East Asia and China.

If you believe and follow the principles of Confucius today, how do you act? You uphold a traditional ethical code of conduct. You embrace learning, especially of human history. You follow the principle of righteous behavior as a gentleman/woman, keeping your focus on virtue in both good times and bad. You believe in the inherent goodness and perfectibility of humankind and social institutions. You respect your parents and elders.

Taoism (or Daoism, as it is increasingly being spelled) believes in humility, the ethical practice of good deeds, and control of one's passions, leading to harmony with the *Tao* (the Way). Taoists believe in meditation to achieve internal and cosmic harmony and seek to create blessings for the individual and the community.

Taoism traces its roots to prehistoric China, but its history as a religion is commonly said to have begun with Lao Tzu, whom many traditionalists date as a contemporary of Confucius. Others believe Lao Tzu was not an actual person, but a literary genre from around 300 BCE. The *Tao Te Ching* (attributed to Lao Tzu) is a 5,500 word book upon which the Taoist philosophy is based. This book is most likely a collection of oral sayings and writings from as early as 200 BCE. They typically are short, cryptic, and subject to innumerable interpretations (could Lao Tzu have been a politician?).

Some see *Tao Te Ching* and its philosophy as a reaction to the rationalism of Confucianism. They see in it a longing to return to a simpler, more tranquil ancient time. Taoists believed in humans as spontaneous creatures of nature and chafed at the Confucianism principles of duty and obligation.

Taoism influenced Buddhism in the form of Zen Buddhism, a fusion of Buddhism and Taoism, that evolved around 500 CE. Taoists didn't quite take to the Buddhist view that suffering must be overcome; to Taoists, suffering was as natural as non-suffering. But when it came to celibacy, monasticism, and the ideas of karma and rebirth, à la Buddhism, Taoists had no problem.

The Tao (the Way) is thought of as nonbeing by some; that is, as the divine Creator of the world. Nonduality is a key principle of the Tao, meaning an integral relationship exists between one thing and its opposite (night and day, joy and sorrow, *yin* and *yang*). This principle can also refer to the return of all things to their origin.

Religious Taoists teach in simple ethical terms the demand of the Tao for moral self-restraint, humility, and unselfishness. They believe transgressions should be punished. Terrible consequences await those profiting at others' expense.

Longevity, or even physical immortality, is thought to result from good conduct. Combining the metals lead (yin) and mercury (yang), was thought to yield gold in an elixir for immortality. Controlled breathing symbolically replaces alchemy and is practiced by Taoists to this day.

Taiwan, Singapore, Thailand, and Indonesia have active Taoist communities, as do other locations with traditionalist Chinese populations. The People's Republic of China once had the largest Taoist religious community, but the Communist regimes stamped out Taoism and other organized religions during the so-called Cultural Revolution of the 1960s. The monasteries and temples became museums and public buildings, and the religion has never recovered its status.

The Taoist tradition is strongest now in Taiwan, where priests are married and pass their esoteric knowledge and ordination to one of their sons. Taiwan Taoist priests perform exorcisms, healings, and great community sacrifices of thanksgiving. They petition for general blessings, inauguration of temples, ordination of priests, and anniversaries. Taoism today is magical, mythical, and ritualistic.

How does a Taoist practice today? Good deeds, humility, and control of one's passions are seen as leading to harmony with the Tao. The Tao is experienced HERE, in every moment of life and especially within nature and the natural world, while the hereafter is seen as little more than, well… an afterthought, at best. Many Taoists meditate in an effort to achieve internal and cosmic harmony. An ancient technique for mental focus called *qigong* teaches how to move energy in subtle channels throughout the body for the purpose of enhancing good health. If you don't want to try this at home, you can always consult your local acupuncturist—another form of Traditional Chinese Medicine.

Taoists seek to create blessings for the individual and the community. They believe that they must act ethically and there are terrible consequences and punishment for personal evil deeds.

# BUDDHISM

*Listen to the teachings of the Awakened One.*

Buddhism follows the eternal truth of Buddha and believes you reach individual perfection by right action toward yourself and others. It includes living by moral virtues and practicing responsible citizenship, as in "love and respect God and your neighbor as yourself."

Buddhism traces its beginning to Siddhartha Gautama, an Indian prince from a small state in what is now Nepal. No biography was written during his lifetime, and only isolated events from his life before he attained enlightenment were preserved. As a result, much of the following is probably mythical in nature.

The Buddha was born a prince in 563 BCE (give or take a hundred years) in the Himalayan foothills (give or take a hundred miles). His father was king of the Sakyas clan. His mother was Maya. The family was Hindu.

Unlike later accounts of Jesus, no one claimed Siddhartha was born of a virgin. But he exited from his mother's side in a sort of painless C-section. The earth shook as he was born (nowadays known as contractions). He supposedly stood up, took seven steps, and announced he would be the "chief of the world" (a little cheeky for an infant), and that this would be his last incarnation.

He is said to have left his wife and young son (now called child abandonment) and their comfy lifestyle at the age of twenty-nine, in search of a solution to the problem of suffering. Vedic Hinduism was the dominant religion of the time, and many serious seekers were willing to undertake the South Beach Diet and other extreme austerities in the pursuit of enlightenment. Siddhartha tried this without success (supposedly gaining five pounds). There must be, he thought, an easier way.

And he persisted until he found it. Reportedly at the age of thirty- five, he became enlightened through a process of meditation and moderation that he called "the Middle Way." After that, (presto-change-o) he was known as the Buddha (enlightened one). He spent the rest of his life preaching his message as he traveled throughout the Ganges Valley. He was known widely as a holy man.

According to Vietnamese Buddhist monk Thich Nhat Hanh, Buddha found the Vedic priests of the time to be hopelessly corrupt and their teaching the cause of much of the social injustice of the day. In reaction to the caste system and the terrible treatment of the untouchables, the Buddha taught the concept of *non-atman* (non-self). To put it bluntly, you, I, and McDonalds don't actually exist.

Asoka, the conquering monarch of India in about 270 BCE, nonetheless campaigned to propagate Buddhism throughout India and Ceylon. In later centuries, it was spread by monks to Kashmir and Southeast Asia. By the seventh century, Buddhism had been well established in China and Korea, and some time later in Japan and in Tibet (ultimately led by the Dalai Lama). During the eleventh century, however, sales figures were off and its numbers declined. On the one hand, Buddhism was all but reabsorbed into Hinduism (the philosophy that you can reach the highest state by leading a simple life in your own home, for example) by the twelfth century. On the other, a number of Buddhists or former Buddhists converted (or were converted) to Islam at this time of Muslim invasion and control. After this period of near extinction in India, Buddhism managed to survive in the surrounding areas and has had a major growth spurt in the twentieth century.

Historically, two main schools of Buddhism developed. A strict and conservative form, Theravada Buddhism, dominated for about a hundred years after the death of the master. It is still found in Thailand, Burma, Cambodia, and Laos. In about the fourth century, Mahayana Buddhism formed around the belief that the ideal of Buddha is open to every being. Mahayana Buddhism is prevalent in China, Japan, Korea, Tibet, and Mongolia.

The word *Buddha* means "to awaken" or "one who has woken up." Buddhists believe most people live their lives asleep, never truly knowing the world around them or seeing life as it really is. As a consequence they suffer. A Buddha is someone who awakens to the knowledge of the world as it is, and so finds release from suffering.

A Buddha teaches out of sympathy and compassion for our suffering and for the benefit and welfare of all beings. Buddhism does not actively look for new followers, but welcomes those who want to try its teaching out for size. Buddhism, like Hinduism, can coexist with other faiths. There are Buddhists who are Christian, for example. Peace and serenity are major goals, and it has been said that no war has ever been fought over Buddhism.

Although Buddhism has the early Pali Canon and the later Mahayana scriptures, it does not have a unique creed; there is no single authority (no Buddha Pope) and no single sacred book like the Torah in Judaism, the Bible in Christianity, or Qur'an in Islam.

Buddhism is not doctrinaire, not wedded to a scriptural doctrine. Thich Nhat Hanh says that for a Buddhist to be attached to any doctrine—even a Buddhist one, such as non-self—is to betray the Buddha.

Buddhism is much more individualistic than are other major world religions, and it focuses on each person seeking to attain enlightenment. It holds that nothing exists permanently. For Buddhists, life is a continuing process of birth and death, but no soul is reborn in this process. All that happens is that one moment gives rise to the next.

One can escape this cycle of suffering by reaching nirvana, or a state of enlightenment. This is done through the eradication of cravings (yes, even for chocolate) by following the Eightfold Path. The path consists of right understanding, right thinking, right speaking, right acting, right lifestyle, right endeavoring, right mindfulness and finally, right contemplation.

Buddhists, though, don't talk much about nirvana because it means the extinction of all notions, concepts, and speech. Rather than spending your time speculating about God or heaven (the hereafter), the Buddhist approach is to live HERE in the present moment with mindful awareness.

Buddhism in the twenty-first century is a large and diverse religion and philosophy, with 380 million followers. Especially over the last sixty years, Buddhism has been growing in the West. Westerners have been attracted to it as a response to materialism and as an opportunity for personal spiritual growth. It is seen as rational and non-dogmatic and as less structured and more in tune with modern science and society than are Western religions. One of the fastest growing forms of Buddhism in the United States is insight meditation, which uses the technique of mindfulness as a key practice.

The essence of Buddhism is following the eternal truth of Buddha, as it manifests HERE in moment-to-moment awareness, and reaching freedom from worldly attachments and desires. Buddhists believe in moderation—the "Middle Path" that led the Buddha to enlightenment. Buddhists have become politically active—in Thailand, Vietnam, and Burma (Myanmar) especially—to achieve social and environmental change without force or violence to others. They typically make friendly, compassionate neighbors, ever mindful of internal and universal peaceful coexistence.

# CHRISTIANITY

*This is the way and Good News of Jesus Christ.*

Christianity believes in a Trinity of Father, Son, and Holy Spirit within one Supreme God. Christians believe we should love our neighbors (friends and enemies) as we love ourselves and families.

Jesus Christ, a historical person, inspired the religion that bears his name. By most accounts, Jesus was a Palestinian populist preacher, and perhaps a Pharisee—a kind of a pre-rabbi. He lived from about the beginning of the modern era until about the year 30 CE. Christians regard Jesus as the Son of God. He is seen as a god–inspired human by many Hindus, as a prophet by Muslims and Baha'is, and by many Jews as a historically significant teacher. Jesus is the most widely known prophet and manifestation of God.

The earliest historians, however, hardly gave Jesus even his fifteen minutes of fame. He was no more than a footnote in the Roman history of that time. Few Judeans had video cams or voice recorders. They literally just remembered for the first couple of generations.

Most current knowledge of Jesus comes from the New Testament Gospels and Epistles, written after two or three generations had come and gone. Little or no knowledge of Jesus comes from so-called disinterested sources, except possibly what we know from the Romans who crucified him. Virtually all other information comes from his devotees—believers in his divinity. Even they claim little knowledge about his family life.

Dunkin' John the Baptist baptized Jesus and greatly influenced him. After John's execution, Jesus continued John's emphasis on preparing for the end of the world and the Kingdom of God soon to come. Jesus reaffirmed the Torah and did not baptize followers into a new sect. It appears he did not intend to start a new religion. Christians, however, regard his association with his apostles as the beginnings of Christianity.

Unlike traditional Jews, the early Christians were missionaries and moved to convert both fellow Jews and gentiles. Saul (the converted

Pharisee, turned Apostle-to-the-gentiles Paul) became the chief proselytizer. He spread the message of salvation-through-Christ in Asia Minor and into parts of Europe. (No evidence exists that he worked on commission.) As Christian gentiles became dominant, they repressed, persecuted, and segregated the Jews. This continued for centuries.

Jesus and his fellow Jews were a minority somewhat tolerated by the Roman occupying government. The history of the Jews had been one of persecution, slavery, and exodus. Their religious and cultural expectation was to be saved as chosen ones by their all-powerful God.

But these same Jews did not have a history of living up to their chosen status. They had sinned often and egregiously, and had been punished by their all-just God. And at the time of Jesus, things were not going smoothly. The Pharisees had lost touch with the message of Moses. Money was being changed in the temple. The rabbis had become a privileged class, in many cases buttering up (technical term) the Roman occupiers.

Jesus did not see himself as divine. He saw himself as a reformer of a corrupted Jewish faith and of the unjust religious practices of his time. He challenged the status quo, seemingly with full knowledge of the personal risks. It would be a big biblical stretch to think he envisioned a new religion, especially the complex organizations now making up Christianity.

After Jesus' death and his reported resurrection, his followers surely needed to believe he was something other than a common crucified criminal. They reasoned no mere man who ministered to the sick and dispossessed could possibly have been guilty as charged by the religious and civil authorities. They became convinced that through Jesus' life and death, God had delivered the salvation promised in the Old Testament. And so the stories of who he was and what he did during his life began to take root and grow.

What happened after he died and was physically gone from this earth? What happened when he was not providing day-to-day guidance— answering the questions and doubts his followers had expressed all through his preaching career? Of course his followers and believers tried to remember and capture what he had said and to remember the spirit and details of how he had lived.

After this oral interpretation period, some forty years after the death of Jesus, his followers began actually recording his life and works. Mark,

Mathew, Luke, and later John, gathered stories and incidents remembered (and presumably sometimes imagined) by those who knew Jesus (or those who knew those who knew), and they started writing these stories down. These Jesus successors, anointed, appointed, or self- described, must have recognized their memories and the memories of other witnesses were beginning to fail, and that already many different accounts of Jesus' history were circulating.

Folks such as the Apostles Peter and Paul saw the absence of the handwriting on the wall. Believers in Jesus and converts from Judaism surely saw the need to get organized. If there was to be a unified, coherent, universal, and organized religion, it was up to the insiders to collect and document the words and life of Jesus. They likely were concerned about the contrasts between reported versions of Jesus' life and their own eye-witness experiences. Even various insiders had differing accounts—not surprising because people see through the filter of their own experience and emotions.

Paul and other early Christians thought of Jesus as the one promised in the Jewish scriptures (only later to be named the Old Testament). These early Christians saw their religion as extending belief in the fulfillment of Judaism. (As Muslims believe the Qur'an clarifies and refines the words of the prophets of Judaism and Christianity; and Baha'is believe their message is a still further refinement). The apostles and early Christians met in the synagogues of Galilee and Jerusalem and generally followed Jewish law and customs.

But missionary life was not for the faint of heart or body. Early Christians were first ignored, then harassed; some were even martyred by the Romans. But it was not just the Christians who were being persecuted during this time. The Jews were fighting for their orthodox cultural and religious lives. The Romans seemed to have a live-and-let-live policy regarding religious sects only as long as they were not a threat to the government and society. Catching the attention of the emperor or the regional authorities was not a good thing.

For the combined reasons of religion and politics, the Jews rebelled against Roman authority. The Zealots, the violently radical Jews, used commando raids against the Romans and even killed Jewish collaborators. And, as they say, the walls came tumbling down. Some Jews blamed the

Zealots, claiming their unwillingness to accede to Roman authority caused the destruction of their temple and the loss of Jerusalem.

It's no wonder Jews were not the best prospects for conversion. In addition to the Roman persecution of the Jews, there grew a Christian dissatisfaction with their fellow chosen folks. Jews were not cooperating with the idea of Jesus as the Messiah. Animosity grew. It became necessary for Christians of this period to explain and account for this script change from what was said when Jesus walked the (Jewish) earth. The story of the Crucifixion, for example, turned into an indictment of not only the Romans, but also into blame for the Jews for not recognizing that the Messiah had come.

The New Testament was written during the time Jews were not cooperating with their conversion. They were being persecuted by the Romans and were generally rejecting Jesus. This had to affect the accounts of the writers of the Gospels.

The rocky road from Galilee all the way to now is marked by potholes and bridge collapses of religious history. Christianity was heresy to Roman civic rituals and to the doctrines of Judaism from which it grew. So did Christian dogma grow out of heresy.

In the year 313, Emperor Constantine of Rome legalized Christianity. Then, in the year 325, he called a worldwide (Ecumenical) conference, the First Council of Nicaea, to squelch differences in developing Church doctrine and practice. The three hundred attending bishops, incidentally, prohibited kneeling during Mass, young female housekeepers for clerics, and self-castration (the latter two were reportedly not related). Regional conferences before, and some after, sharply disagreed with many of the key decisions. Nonetheless, this conference determined the basic beliefs and doctrines of the Church. Theodosius in 380 made Christianity the official religion of the Roman Empire.

This official state recognition became a blessing and a curse. In one sense, Christianity triumphed over the Roman Empire. But in another sense, the Empire took over and the Church succumbed to the established civil order. Some say this is when Christianity became akin to citizenship rather than choice.

In 393, a council known as the Synod of Hippo listed the basic acceptable text, chapters, and form of today's Bible. Although there had been many early versions of Christianity, the Saint Paul (of Epistle fame) version won out over the Gnostic (do-we-really-need-the-Church?) Gospels version, its chief competitor.

A cataclysmic schism (worse than when the Beatles broke up) came in 1054, when the Pope of the West (Leo IX) and the Patriarch of the East (Michael I) excommunicated each other, dividing Christianity to the present day. This date only marks the end of an extended disagreement over the primacy of the Pope. In other words, who gets to be the boss of the whole Church?

The other key issue was the unilateral addition of the three words "and the Son" to the text of the Nicene Creed, which the Church had adopted as a statement of correct belief in 325 CE. These words reinforced the Roman Catholic version of the Trinity, but this language addition was rejected by the Eastern Church, and is still being debated today.

The Roman and the Eastern Churches each insist the other abandoned the true faith and that they alone are the one, true, catholic (universal), holy, and apostolic Church. The Roman and Eastern Churches rescinded the excommunications in 1965, a scant 911 years after the original spat, and in 2005 officials of Eastern Churches attended the funeral of Pope John Paul II in Rome. Although the spirit of reconciliation is in the air, consider that the high-level bureaucracies of both Churches would likely have to shrink by half if they again became a single Church. (Like modern government shrinking by half?)

In the sixteenth century, Martin Luther, a Roman Catholic monk, jump-started the Reformation with his demands for reform. He maintained the independence of individual believers and that the Bible, not the Pope, was the primary authority for Christians. As a result, the Western division of Christianity further divided into Pope-centric Roman Catholicism and Protestantism.

Each denomination of Protestantism has different views of rituals, practices, and beliefs, but all consider themselves Christians. To this day, individual freedom and moral responsibility, reliance on the Bible and faith alone (as opposed to faith and good works), and rejection of the Pope in favor of governance by all believers are some common Protestant characteristics.

The expansion and growth (some forced) of Christianity have continued to the present. Today about 2.1 billion people identify themselves as Christians, the largest number worldwide for any organized religion. In 2001, the *World Christian Encyclopedia* listed 34,000 different Christian groups identified across the globe. Protestant denominations account for as many as six hundred million (some thirty percent of all Christians).

Among the many Christian groups, Pentecostals and charismatic Christians are two very similar movements. They both believe contemporary Christians should experience the Holy Spirit much as the earliest Christians did—through miracles, for example.

The key characteristic of **Pentecostals** (from the early 1900s) is that they must undergo baptism of the Holy Spirit following a traditional baptism. Primary evidence that the follow-up conversion actually took is the experience of glossolalia, or speaking in tongues. With as many as five hundred million practitioners, Pentecostalism is the world's fastest-growing Christian group. Pentecostalism accommodates local rites and traditions and offers an emotionally based theology. The absence of a strict church hierarchy appeals to many.

**Charismatic** is the name given to the spread of Pentecostalism within the mainline Christian churches in the 1960s. Charismatics share much theology with Pentecostals, but tend to remain with their original denominations. Baptists, Catholics, Methodists, and Episcopalians have all joined the movement in some numbers.

**Evangelicals** make up a broader, older classification of Christians, dating from the Reformation. This group referred at different times to Lutherans, Anglicans, slavery abolitionists, and to the revivalists of the early 1800s. They feel it is their duty to lead others to salvation through Jesus Christ. The stresses of industrialization and their reaction to Darwin's *Origin of the Species* led some evangelicals to Christian fundamentalism, a form of evangelism that retreated from the social agenda of general evangelism and embraced a literal interpretation of the Bible. Today, Protestant evangelism includes such diverse groups as black Baptists, Southern Baptists, Dutch Reformed Churches, Mennonites and Pentecostals, and Catholic charismatics. There are an estimated 480 million evangelicals worldwide.

Catholics, Protestants of all sorts, evangelicals, and Christians in general through the ages have been missionaries. One thing that has changed over time is that at least some Christians today take a softer line, expressing respect for the beliefs and customs of other cultures and religions before converting their sorry native, pagan, heathen, heretic, or wrong-denomination asses.

Many schisms, heresies, sects, and denominations sprang from the original messages of Jesus. But the ancient Bible compiled and validated in the years 100 through 400 remains largely intact today. This early Bible was divided into the Old Testament (Hebrew Bible) and the New Testament, which detailed the teachings of Jesus. It sums up these teachings as follows:

The commandments, "You shall not commit adultery; you shall not kill; you shall not steal; you shall not covet," and whatever other commandment there may be, are summed up in this saying, [namely] "You shall love your neighbor as yourself." Love does no evil to the neighbor; hence, love is the fulfillment of the law. (Paul to the Romans 13: 9-10)

The Bible, however, did not rely solely on love to keep the social order. Another passage in Paul's Letter to the Romans provides this advice (and guiding IRS principle):

Let every person be subordinate to the higher [civil] authorities, for there is no authority except from God, and those that exist have been established by God. Therefore, whoever resists authority opposes what God has appointed…. This is also why you pay taxes, for the authorities are ministers of God. (Paul to the Romans 13: 1-6)

For those who take a literal interpretation of the Bible, this and similar passages are hard to explain away:

Slaves are to be under the control of their masters in all respects, giving them satisfaction, not talking back to them or stealing from them, but exhibiting complete good faith, so as to adorn the doctrine of God our savior in every way. (Titus 3: 9-10)

As well as, "Slaves, be obedient to your human masters with fear and trembling" (Ephesians 6: 5) and "As the church is subordinate to Christ, so wives should be subordinate to their husbands in everything" (Ephesians 5: 24). Thankfully, most Christians nowadays don't believe slavery and male domination were the Jesus message. Instead, they're willing to recognize the biblical addendums of certain early male "interpreters."

Jesus spoke to a particular audience—in most cases, an illiterate audience. He was reported to be wise, but not a writer and not literate himself. Somewhat like (no offense intended) certain politicians and movie stars or TV personalities, he spoke the common language and connected with audiences in a special way. In spite of biblical language grafted on later to justify the taking of slaves and a male hierarchy, Jesus captured peoples' imagination with a message that spoke to their souls— to their best instincts. He spoke to the oppressed and downtrodden.

Although Christians today come in more than 34,000 sizes and shapes, most still share these basic beliefs:

> There is only one God.
> God has created the world as distinct from Himself, but is believed to be active within it.
> Humans are created at a distance from God and are responsible for their own lives. God is judge of all they do, but also seeks to help them when they go wrong.
> God reveals Himself in the Trinity.

Most Christians believe Jesus came to earth as a man-God to restore the failed relationship between humans and God. Jesus was crucified as a criminal in sacrifice and atonement for man's sins and was reportedly seen alive after he was dead and buried.

Christians believe the main purpose of Jesus' life was to teach people how to be reconciled to God and to each other; and to live their lives according to his example.

They believe they have only one life, which is judged after death by the way they lived. In other words, how well they put Jesus' message of love into practice HERE on earth determines their fate in the hereafter. Heaven awaits those who lived a good life; eternal punishment in hell awaits those who led a bad life. Whether heaven and hell literally exist is hotly debated in theological circles.

Christians believe Jesus preached about acts of love.

# ISLAM

*Surrender yourself totally to God.*

Islam believes in a Supreme God who is to be respected and worshiped and shown gratitude. "There is no God but God, and Muhammad is his Prophet" is the Islam statement of faith. Muslims believe they have an obligation to their fellow humans, especially those who are less fortunate.

Islam was founded by Muhammad, who is held to be the "Seal of the Prophets," or the last of the prophets who began with Adam.

Muhammad was born about the year 570, in Mecca, in what is now Saudi Arabia, into a poor clan of the dominant tribe Quraish. His father, Abdullah, died while his mother Amina was pregnant, and she died shortly after his birth. His uncle Abu Talib became his guardian. Muhammad is the next most widely known prophet after Jesus.

He became materially successful, at least partially because of his business association and subsequent marriage to the rich widow Khadija. She supported him in many ways and gave him social standing. He had four sons who died in infancy and four daughters.

Muhammad was spiritually inspired, in part, by appreciation and gratitude for his uncommon good fortune. He apparently began his spiritual quest within the customs of his own polytheistic tribe, but broke with that tradition to become a monotheist. He was likely influenced, as well, by the local Jewish community and by the Christian missionary efforts in his neighborhood. Abraham, the prophet of the Jews, is also claimed as the first Muslim and the patriarch of all Muslims through his son Ishmael. As Christianity incorporated Judaism, so Islam incorporated Judaism and Christianity. Both built on the earlier prophets and scriptures.

Following the custom of religious retreat, Muhammad liked to go to the mountain of Hira, near Mecca. During one of these monthly retreats, he had his first religious experience, in the form of inspiration. He later saw visions of the Angel Gabriel, who is described as the bearer of God's revelations to Muhammad. These revelations occurred between the years 610 and 630.

Muhammad believed his role as Prophet was to remind humankind (at least his Arab world) that God (Allah) had been generous to them. In return for Allah's generosity, they had obligations to Allah and their fellow humans.

As with Jesus, Muhammad was at first discounted by leaders in his society; in this case, in Mecca. Like Jesus, Muhammad became a social and economic threat when folks realized he preached fundamental change to their cherished traditions. The Meccan leadership became nervous when they realized he was gathering a substantial band of followers.

Muhammad was protected for a time by the social standing of his guardian uncle and by his wife. When they both died, his enemies—supporters of the traditional, commercially viable religious order—were emboldened, and an economic boycott was imposed upon this troublemaker. In about 622, for financial and safety reasons, Muhammad and his followers migrated from Mecca to the town of Medina. Muhammad used his highly regarded mediation and leadership skills to resolve local factional differences. Soon he had joined and was leading the Medina body politic.

To help support his displaced followers, Muhammad successfully conducted a raid against a Meccan trade caravan. Superior Meccan forces fought Muhammad at Badr and lost, prompting an all-out Meccan campaign to capture Medina, which failed. Mecca was ultimately peacefully conquered by Muhammad in about 630, shortly before his death in 632. His final great act was a pilgrimage to the reformed shrine Ka'ba. This pilgrimage, the *Hajj*, is re-enacted annually by millions of modern-day Muslims.

Muhammad's entire life and religious experiences are chronicled in the Qur'an (sometimes written Koran in English), the Islamic equivalent of the Christian Bible. The revelations were orally passed to rememberers, until around twenty years after Muhammad's death. Then, the oral (and maybe some written elements) were transcribed and collected into the single definitive Arabic text.

The Qur'an is thought to be the untranslatable-from-Arabic, direct word of God, as dictated by God and relayed to Muhammad. In this text, Muslims hear God speaking in His own words. These words are thought to be a miracle and have become the comprehensive daily guide for correct Muslim behavior, as well as a complete vision of both history and destiny. The Qur'an gives no human agency the right to interpret the message. Believers are personally accountable at Judgment Day to have interpreted the message for themselves.

Two main sects or subdivisions of Islam developed. These groups are the Sunnis and the Shi'as (or Shi'ites). Immediately after Muhammad's death, a power struggle erupted between Ali, his cousin and son-in-law, with whom he was raised as a brother, and his father-in-law, Abu Bakr. The Shi'as believed Ali was Muhammad's designated successor, and the Sunnis went with Bakr. Even today, Sunnis adhere to the *sunnah* (behavior or practice) of Muhammad in Medina, and to the hadith (the entire body of text of Muslim tradition). The Shi'as (literally, separate party) follow a line of *imams* (leaders) they consider direct descendants of Muhammad and consider the word of an imam to be absolute.

Based on the Iranian revolution, the West thinks of Shi'ism as fundamentalist. However, Shi'as have become sophisticated rationalists, with a strong political commitment against the privileged ruling establishment.

The religion of Muhammad—Islam—is now the world's second most widely followed religion. From its original form 1400 years ago in Arabia, it swiftly became a world faith, and now has around 1.3 billion adherents (about eighty-five percent Sunni and fifteen percent Shi'ite). Pakistan, Bangladesh, and India claim 550 million followers; Malaysia and Indonesia 150 million. Africa has some 330 million and China some 30 million.

Surprising to most Westerners, Arab Muslims are estimated at only fifteen percent of the total, or about 180 million. In officially Muslim countries, such as Saudi Arabia, Pakistan, and Malaysia, unless they register otherwise, individual citizens/residents are Muslim by nationality. Most Muslims do not belong to churches or religious bodies in the sense most Christians do.

Islam is closely associated with the prevalent culture. For a person in a Muslim country to identify as anything but Muslim has serious negative social repercussions, perhaps even dangerous physical consequences. Rejecting one's religion, apostasy, is not such a big deal in most other faiths. For Muslims, however, rejection of the belief in Allah or the practice of Islam can be punishable by death. This is a strong inducement to self-identify as a loyal and devoted follower of the faith.

Inability to easily leave the Islam faith probably skews the numbers of reported believers. The same is somewhat true, though, for any family/ socially sanctioned religion—that is, all the world's major faiths. Social pressures to conform may have some of the same inhibiting effects as do the physical pressures to remain attached to the religious party line.

Sunni Muslims may actually outnumber Catholics in terms of daily practice of religious rituals. Millions of devout Muslims voluntarily and enthusiastically practice their faith. But let the death contract (fatwa) on Salman Rushdie be an example to anyone who thinks of straying from the public profession of their Muslim birthright.

*Islam* is an Arabic word meaning "surrendering oneself to the will of God, and achieving peace and security by doing so." A person surrenders to the will of Allah by living and thinking in the way Allah has instructed.

Thus, Islam is more than a system of religious beliefs. More formal and perhaps more strict than most other religions, Islam is a comprehensive set of life directives. The Islamic faith provides a complex social and legal system that governs family life, law and order, ethics, dress, and cleanliness, as well as religious ritual and observance.

Muslims are expected to pray five times daily, facing in the direction of Mecca, and to make a pilgrimage to Mecca (the Hajj) at least once in their lifetime. They should also "bear witness," meaning they sincerely and publicly declare, "There is no god but God, and Muhammad is the Prophet of God." These and other basic Muslim obligations are known collectively as the Five Pillars of Islam.

Muslim doctrine is summarized in Six Articles of Faith (sometimes narrowed to five), which state that a Muslim must believe in and submit to the will of one Supreme God, as well as believe in His angels and prophets (first among them, Muhammad), and in the Qur'an.

Islam doesn't have a church or clergy or pope, but has sheiks, mullahs, or imams who, like rabbis or priests, give counsel, conduct marriages, and perform last rites. Their opinions and fatwas, are persuasive but not binding. Individual due diligence is expected to sort out what is the will of God.

The Qur'an is the primary source of Islamic law because Muslims believe this is literally God speaking through the Prophet Muhammad. Muslims also follow the example set by Muhammad's life, as revealed through the sunnah; the precedents of old legal cases and consensus of jurors; and some say, Muslims in general.

The Qur'an talks of Adam and Eve, Abraham and his sons, Noah and the flood, and many of the figures in the Old and New Testament. It acknowledges other faiths (Peoples of the Book), saying, "The [Muslim] believers, the Jews, the Christians...—all those who believe in God and the Last Day and do good—will have their rewards with their Lord" (sura 2: aya 62). It even goes so far as to say,

> We [Muslims] believe in God and in what has been sent down to us and to Abraham, Ishmael, Isaac, Jacob, and the Tribes. We believe in what has been given to Moses, Jesus, and the prophets from their Lord. We do not make a distinction between any of the [prophets]. It is to Him that we devote ourselves. (sura 3: aya 84, 85)

Westerners sometimes believe Islam is inherently violent, in part because some modern extremists are violent, and in part because of the statement in the Qur'an that says, "Slay them wherever you find them" (sura 2: aya 191). However, "them" can be understood to refer to "those who attack you." According to M. A. S. Abdel Haleem's interpretation, "The prevalent message of the Qur'an is one of peace and tolerance but it allows self-defense."

Adding to the perception of aggressiveness of the Muslim faith is the so-called sword verse: "When the [four] forbidden months are over, wherever [in or outside the Sanctuary in Mecca] you find the polytheists, kill them, seize them, besiege them, ambush them" (sura 9: aya 5).

However, in context, the "pagan" establishment of the era reportedly broke its treaty and sought to convert back Muslims, killing or expelling those who did not recant their faith. So this passage was a Muslim declaration of war in defense of their faith and physical well-being. Note that this sword verse is followed by an order to grant safe harbor to those enemies seeking it, and exempts polytheists who keep the peace with Muslims. Although some extremist Muslims interpret this passage as a general, inherent call to war and violence, it seems to refer instead to a particular time and place.

The term *jihad* is commonly translated as "fighting," but can also be translated as "struggle," according to Haleem. *The Perennial Dictionary of World Religions* says, "Jihad can mean 'holy war,' but the struggle for uprightness of life and the propagation of the faith prefers peaceful means such as persuasion and example."

Of course, extremist suicide bombers see it differently. They think literally when they read,

> [Prophet], do not think of those who have been killed in God's way as dead. They are alive with their Lord, well provided for, happy with what God has given them of His favour; rejoicing that for those they have left behind who have yet to join them there is no fear, nor will they grieve. (sura 3: aya 169, 170)

And:

> Their Lord has answered them: "I will not allow the deeds of any one of you to be lost, whether you are male or female, each is like the other [in rewards]. I will certainly wipe out the bad deeds of those who emigrated and were driven out of their homes, who suffered harm for My cause, who fought and were killed. I will certainly admit them to Gardens graced with flowing streams [where they will have everything they wish (16: 31) including good- natured, beautiful maidens 55: 70] as a reward from God: the best reward is with God." (sura 3: aya 195)

The Qur'an seems, however, to draw a distinction between being killed in the service of Allah (typically in self-defense or in a just war) and killing oneself. The verse that says, "Spend in God's cause: do not contribute to your destruction with your own hands, but do good, for God loves those who do good" (sura 2: aya 195) can be interpreted to outlaw suicide or any form of self-injury.

It is a little harder to argue gender equity from the words of the Qur'an, as well as from the actions of a few fundamentalist Muslim societies today, such as that of Saudi Arabia. For example, the Qur'an refers to the testimony of one man equaling that of two female witnesses:

> Call in two men as witnesses. If two men are not there, then call one man and two women out of those you approve as witnesses, so that if one of the two women should forget [or err] the other can remind her. (sura 2: aya 282)

Haleem advises us to take the verse in the context of the importance of recording debt in writing, not testimony in general. He also notes the practical fact that, at the time, women were generally less literate than men were. Muhammad had very high regard for his wife, Khadija, as his partner, advisor, and companion, suggesting a very practical and meaningful respect for women (at least for his time).

Describing the current moderate form or "lived Islam," Khaled Abou El Fadl notes that Muslim women in most places choose whether or not to wear a veil, attend universities, and practice the professions. They are not restricted from contact with men at work or in leisure activities. Today a woman is governor of an Afghanistan province. In Pakistan, Benazir Bhutto was twice elected prime minister, and the tragedy of her assassination and riotous response only underscores the changing Muslim attitude toward women.

Like many modern world religions, Islam claims it represents and is the keeper of the exclusive and pre-eminent word of God:

> It was He who sent His Messenger with guidance and the religion of Truth to show that [Islam] is above every [other] religion. God suffices as a witness: Muhammad is the Messenger of God. Those who follow him are harsh towards the disbelievers and compassionate towards each other." (sura 48: aya 28, 29)

Diverging interpretations of the faith developed after the death of Muhammad, similar to the confusion after the death of Jesus. Apparently some of the Qur'an was written and perhaps edited and approved by Muhammad prior to his death in the year 632. Or at least he approved of some of the oral versions entrusted to "rememberers." Most historians agree Muhammad himself did not write at all. So it wasn't until some twenty years after Muhammad died that the passages of the Qur'an began to be assembled by order of Caliph Uthman.

By then, different interpretations had arisen. Unfortunately, Muhammad had not designated a tie breaker to resolve any deadlocked disputes about authenticity. To insure uniformity and orthodoxy, Uthman ordered unofficial Qur'an versions burned. Likely, the same conditions existed as when the Christian Gospels were written; that is, memories faded after some years, and the religious leaders saw the need to record an official version of the Qur'an.

This documentation of Islam took place during a particularly turbulent period, which saw the Muslim conquest of Syria, Iraq, Persia, Egypt, all of North Africa, and much of Central Asia. Shortly after proclaiming the official version of the Qur'an, Caliph Uthman was assassinated, setting off the first Muslim civil war. This war brought Ali to power and began a Muslim history of three political dynasties: the Ottoman Empire in Turkey, the Middle East, and Mediterranean; the Safavid in Iran; and the Mogul in India.

Three of the first four caliphs were assassinated and this period was fraught with expansion and development pains. Arabism developed (most of the conquered Muslim empire was non-Arab), perhaps to facilitate the distribution of booty from extensive conquest, and perhaps as a consequence of a "we were here and we believed first" attitude. Four distinct schools of Islamic law, followed by *madrasa*, the system of religious education, cemented the Arab dominance.

What is the universal truth of Islam? Certainly it is belief in and surrender to one Supreme Being, an all-powerful God who is to be respected and worshiped. Gratitude is shown to God through acts of kindness and compassion HERE and now, which determines our fate in the hereafter. The Qur'an is the handbook for Muslim daily living.

# BAHA'I

*Live in the unity of God, religion, and mankind.*

Baha'i believes in one God who is all wise, and believes we are one world people and should treat each other accordingly. Baha'u'llah, the religious name of the founder of Baha'i, was born in Teheran in 1817, the son of a noble Persian family. He was an early convert and follower of Báb (literally "gateway"), the founder of the Bábi religion. The Baha'is believe Báb to be the return of the prophet Elijah, John the Baptist, and the Twelfth Imam, and believe Báb to be the Prophet Herald of Baha'u'llah. Founder Baha'u'llah is regarded by Baha'is as the most recent in the ancient line of messengers of God that includes Abraham, Moses, Buddha, Jesus, and especially Muhammad.

In the early 1850s, Báb was executed and his followers, including Baha'u'llah, were first imprisoned then exiled to Baghdad. A forty-year exodus (remember Moses, who wouldn't stop and ask for directions?) followed in Constantinople, Turkey, and Acre in Palestine.

Baha'u'llah's many writings are considered revelation to his followers, and his most important book, *Kitáb-i-Aqdas*, contains detailed instructions for Baha'i daily life (as does the Qur'an for Muslims). The Baha'i holy writings reiterate many of the eternal truths spoken by all the divine messengers: the unity of God, love of one's neighbor, and the moral purpose of life. For Baha'is, the hereafter is not a literal location, but a means for the soul to draw closer to God.

At present, the worldwide community of some five to six million Baha'is represents most nations, races, and cultures on earth. It seeks the unification of one global society breaking down traditional barriers of race, class, and creed. However, the Baha'i faith has been rejected by some Muslims, even though it originated as an outgrowth of Islam. Baha'is have been discriminated against by these Muslims and are severely repressed in Iran. Nevertheless, the religion expanded during the mid-1900s as a result of efforts to gain more members. These efforts continue in the form of various multi-year plans. This expansion is viewed as consistent with Baha'i philosophy, as expressed by Baha'u'llah: "The earth is but one country, and mankind its citizens."

Baha'i scriptures, even though dating only to the mid-1800s, suffer from interpretation in today's terms. Some seem sexist, such as one that designates males as heirs, but not females and another that permits polygamy. Even personal hygiene is detailed. But some Baha'i passages come across as universal, such as this one:

Should anyone wax angry with you, respond to him with gentleness; and should anyone upbraid you, forbear to upbraid him in return, but leave him to himself and put your trust in God, the omnipotent Avenger, the Lord of might and justice.

Baha'is believe earlier founders of separate religious systems had the common purpose of bringing the human race to spiritual and moral maturity. They think the human family has now become mature enough for us to have a peaceful global society. They teach tolerance and respect for other beliefs and actively support elimination of prejudice, particularly against women. Their goal is a universal society through universal education and the elimination of the extremes of poverty and wealth.

# NONE OF THE ABOVE

*Faith in religion is not the only faith.*

The world's major religions account for about 5.5 billion of the earth's 7 billion people. What about the categories of "non-religious," "other," "non-affiliated," or simply "none of the above"?

People do not consider secular, atheist, or agnostic as defining religion in any sense of the word. But almost a billion folks on this planet identify themselves as non-religious. And they probably number many more. Those who are polling subjects (victims?) generally tell you what they think you want to hear. And being religious is socially acceptable.

To minimize this social desirability bias, Harris conducted an anonymous, online national poll in 2003. It found twenty-one percent of those raised Catholic, fifty-two percent of those raised Jewish, and ten percent of those raised Protestant, regardless of church attendance, said they do not believe in God or are not sure God exists. These percentages may not extrapolate to world numbers, but clearly there are a large number of non-religious people in the world beyond those who *say* they are non-religious. The same survey indicated half of Americans go to church only a few times a year or never (and Americans attend more often than do folks in most other developed countries).

Do the non-religious (admitted or not) behave better or worse than the religious? And how many church members don't buy some key beliefs or practices of their religion?

If you believe Jesus was a holy prophet but only human (not God), are you a Christian? Are you Catholic if you don't believe the Pope is infallible, if you practice birth control, or if you're divorced? Are you a Muslim if you believe in one God, Allah, and his Prophet Muhammad, but believe revelation continues in every era and Muhammad was not the final prophet? Are you a Protestant if you believe and have faith in God, but believe human good works are also needed for salvation?

Let me tell you about my (raised-) Catholic/Jewish friend Ben, who at age fifty avoids all organized religion. His observation of "the order and organization of the universe" leads him to believe in a higher Spiritual Being. However, he thinks the doctrines and rituals of organized religion were mostly made up.

He points to the parallel propaganda inherent in government "news": he has compared personal observation with written news accounts and discovered many inconsistencies and distortions. Observing the spin of recent history and the conflicting accounts of ancient history, he concludes all church history is imperfect and tainted by the bias of the writers. He can't believe the literal story of Jesus.

Ben practices no organized religion and is offended by religious zealots and by the devoutly intolerant. His friends are mostly tolerantly religious. But he's careful not to express his views because he knows of no organized religion that respects his secularism. He says he might be a Buddhist if pressed—but he doesn't feel pressed.

Ben quietly disapproves of organized religion's great wealth. Most familiar with Roman Catholicism, he notes the enormous wealth of the Church is not diminished by child support payments, nor diluted by pesky heirs, because priests can't marry. (Unplanned hush money to the sexually abused, however, has diminished church wealth.) He wonders what majestic cathedrals have to do with Jesus' message of Christian charity.

Evil done in the name of religion troubles him. He points to the Crusades, Inquisition, and Holocaust as examples of intolerance by and toward religions.

Though un-religious, Ben is a kind, thoughtful, loving, and peaceful human being. Karma and the Golden Rule (do unto others as you would have them do unto you) guide his life. He does "what's right" because "it feels good" and because he believes in the goodness of all people. His children are likewise kind and empathetic. He's a responsible citizen and generous to charities. He obeys civil law, doesn't drink or smoke, and is true to his wife. Ben believes he acts this way because he was "raised with love." He and his wife believe their children act in the same loving way because they, too, are being raised with love.

What motivates Ben? Can this man not "of the Book" be "saved"? (He doesn't worry about being saved, mind you.) Ben believes in God, but not in heaven (though he'd like to), and is glad not to believe in hell.

How would Ben be judged here and now or hereafter by the God of the Christians, Muslims, or Jews?

Another younger friend, Jeanie, was raised Catholic, but says she'd mark "other" on a census form asking for her religion. She believes in a Higher Power, or something beyond mere science, but not in an all- seeing, involved-in-our-lives kind of God. She certainly would not subscribe to the concept of a vengeful God. Jeanie and her husband have talked about how they would expose their children to God. They will not baptize their two children, nor will they advocate an organized religion. They will be honest about not buying the concepts of heaven and hell, but will "expose the kids to various beliefs" and let them decide. Her friends think the way she does.

Jeanie could be described as non-religious. Yet she and her husband lead moral and ethical lives, perhaps more than some do in organized religions. They deserve an eternal reward for a life well lived on earth, but can they go to heaven even if they don't believe in it?

My sister Mary Ann calls herself a Now-ist, which pretty much conveys her judgment of historical religions. She thinks organized religions are training wheels in the bicycle ride of life. She lives very much in the present.

She says, "I believe life is bliss. I'm constantly looking for useful, purposeful, spontaneous moves in a direction that's nourishing." She practices Transcendental Meditation (TM), and is a devotee of the late Maharishi Mahesh Yogi. TM for her has opened a path toward enlightenment. She studies Ayurveda, the traditional medicine of India.

Mary Ann follows the Golden Rule. I find her to be kind, generous, and thoughtful. She is a great sister, aunt, and spouse. She often helps others "manage the challenge of being alive." Although not religious in any organized, establishment sense of the word, she deserves to go to heaven. She would say she's already in heaven.

On a more-famous-than-us scale, Abraham Lincoln is considered one of the most moral leaders ever in the United States. And he was generally known as non-religious. Actually, according to some, he was considered a deist—a person who relies on logic and reason to arrive at the existence of God. Lincoln apparently did not put much stock in the revelations and traditions of organized religions, Christian or any other. Like many politicians then and now, he did sometimes attend church. And he knew how to turn a good religious phrase at the right moment.

Perhaps these personal stories demonstrate that our world's society and organized religions define religion too narrowly. Most people think in practical, day-to-day terms. They equate religion with the major world religions, but with many personal variations. They may share some of the same lofty goals and values of one or more religious groups, yet not consider themselves members of any group.

Let's look at some groups to which they might be said to belong.

**Atheism** is the denial of the existence of a Supreme Being. It is not well organized and is more a simple philosophy, without consistent leadership or ritual. Some label it *rationalism*.

A young friend, Richard, quietly confesses to being an atheist, but really his beliefs would more accurately be classified as fitting with **agnosticism**. The God he doesn't believe in is the God up in heaven, surrounded by angels tooting horns and playing harps. Richard can't identify with the classic paintings showing God with a long white beard and flowing robes. He believes any so-called miracles that demonstrate the power of God can be explained by science. He thinks the Bible and the Qur'an are mostly fabrications to control society and do not at all prove the existence of God. He is not sure Jesus even existed in history, and if he did exist, he was human, not God.

But not believing in a storybook God is not the same as not believing in God at all. Richard admits he just doesn't know or understand about God. He says to argue without doubt that no God exists would be like the fundamentalists' absolute conviction that God *does* exist, and that they know what He looks like and what He is thinking.

Agnostics believe the existence of God cannot be known or demonstrated for certain, but don't argue God cannot possibly exist. No one mistakes agnosticism for organized religion.

**Secularism** is similarly a non-religious philosophy. It is characterized by a focus on the human and worldly and material, rather than on the spiritual and divine.

**Humanism** dates to The *Human Manifesto,* authored in 1933 by Curtis Reese and others. A Unitarian minister, Reese puts it succinctly: God is "philosophically possible, scientifically unproved and religiously unnecessary."

Sam Smith, former editor of the alternative Washington publication *Progressive Review* (and he now continues *Undernews* in email format with regular updates to his website) believes faith in religion is just one kind of faith. He calls atheism the faith in evidence; agnosticism the faith in doubt; science the faith in logic; and "deep ecology" the belief in creation rather than a creator. He says that all deserve the same respect we give organized religions.

The modern-day materialistic United States may be the most secular population on the planet. Yet many evangelical Christians see the United States as a Christian country founded on Christian principles. Neither perception is entirely true.

America does largely self-identify as Christian. But it actually was founded on deist principles (belief in a rational and impersonal God who is not involved in our day-to-day lives). The framers of the U.S. Constitution were wary of—and, in some cases, hostile toward— organized religion.

The Constitution intentionally does not mention God. Article One of the Bill of Rights, enacted in the first session of Congress, lists as the first liberty that "Congress shall make no law respecting an establishment of religion ." In 1801, Jefferson called this the "wall of separation between church and state." In a letter to Horatio G. Spafford, on March 17, 1814, Jefferson writes, "In every country and in every age, the priest has been hostile to liberty. He is always in alliance with the despot, abetting his abuses in return for protection to his own."

The founding fathers first distinguished between God and religion in the language of the Declaration of Independence. They refer to the "Creator," the "Supreme Judge of the world," and the "protection of divine Providence," but not once to God or Jesus Christ.

Yet we call ourselves a Christian nation today: eighty-five percent of Americans said so in the year 2005. Just eleven percent (thirty-two million) said they were non-Christian, agnostic, or non-religious.

If the concept of God is not central to someone's life or if doubts are not pressing, it's easier and simpler just to identify with the family traditional religion. Most of us are born into our family's religion; that is where we seem to stay. Some, especially young people, reject the family religion, but don't replace it with anything else

According to Gallup, which polls Americans annually about their church attendance habits, rates have remained at about forty percent in the past decade. However, actual church attendance and attendance reported to pollsters are not the same. Researchers reporting in *The Christian Century* in 1998 did their own study in one county in Ohio and in another county in Canada, and found the percentage of Christians attending religious services was half that reported in national polls. They theorized this disparity results from a "churched identity" adults hang onto tightly once it's developed. They no longer feel a need to attend church regularly in order to keep up the identity. But they don't mind exaggerating their church attendance when asked.

In other words, people shade the truth to look or sound better. People want other people to see them as church-going believers in God and all things good. So, church membership and spiritual beliefs may well be overstated. And as if social pressure isn't enough, organized religions have an even stronger persuader. They know where we live.

How many members would leave if they thought they could—without forever burning in hell? Even if you doubt whether or not there is a hell or a final judgment, do you really want to take the chance? It's easier just to go along with the rituals and pretend to believe. Who's going to know? Or maybe you believe in public and only doubt in private.

Some friends and relatives of mine took the non-scientific poll on the multi-faith Beliefnet.com website. The Belief-O-Matic showed major disparities between born-into, self-identified religious affiliation and actual personal daily beliefs and practices. This test correlates official doctrine and beliefs of twenty-seven recognized religions with the test taker's beliefs and practices, and assigns a score. A hundred percent means your beliefs perfectly align with a particular religion.

One Catholic friend endured sixteen years of Catholic schooling, sang in the choir, and taught Sunday school. He calls himself a Roman Catholic and claims he took this online test and answered as honestly as possible. He searched the test results, through twenty-six possible choices, all the way to the bottom of the list. There, at number twenty-seven, he found Roman Catholic, with only a seventeen percent correlation between his beliefs and those of the Church. Other friends and relatives had similar and just as dramatic results. Skeptical? Try it. It is free and takes just a few minutes and the results are confidential, unless you care to share.

A more general and scientific survey by the Pew Research Center was released in March 2002. It suggests Americans take a broad and liberal approach to religion and morality. Contrary to the common wisdom, only eighteen percent said they believed theirs is the one true faith. Seventy-five percent believed that "many religions can lead to eternal life." Just under half (forty-seven percent) responded that belief in God is necessary to be moral; however, as many as eighty-seven percent believe one can be a good American even if he or she does not have a religious faith.

Worldwide, the number of none-of-the-above people is approaching a billion: 769 million non-religious and 152 million atheists. That's one out of every six or seven people. In a related trend, Independent now ranks as the second largest category of Christians, after Roman Catholics. So, even within organized faiths, people are moving away from the monolithic, traditional world religions. This all suggests the trend may be more toward secular/non-religious and independent belief and practice than anyone imagined.

Does it matter if the actual numbers of church attendance are half or less than half of the reported numbers? What do the large numbers of non-religious mean? Should one belong to or leave a religion (or non-religion) based on its reported numbers of members? Should one leave a belief (or non-belief) without first finding a better place to go?

Religions are changing, people are changing. Yet, in subtle ways, religions are returning to their roots—as we come to understand and believe that the great world faiths are more alike than different. The centuries' accumulation of ritual and dogma are being stripped away. The outdated dos and don'ts are being discarded. Folks are discovering universal amazing graces in many non-religious places.

Reform is in the air. Bishop Spong says, "Christianity must change or die." Karen Armstrong expands Western thinking with *Muhammad*. A vision, albeit cautious, of Islamic reform is emerging through Reza Aslan's *No god but God* and Shirin Ebadi's Nobel acceptance speech. Atheists, too, are making a public splash with books such as *The God Delusion*, by Richard Dawkins, and *God Is Not Great: How Religion Poisons Everything*, by Christopher Hitchens. Another is *Letter to a Christian Nation,* by Sam Harris. In religion today, everything and nothing are sacred.

Some talk of the clash of civilizations when referring to the contest of ideas between Christianity and Islam. Peace and war may very well hang in the balance. More than global warming (if we are still around), more than national elections, and affecting the lives of millions, is the issue of freedom to choose spirituality in the twenty-first century and beyond. The nascent reforms, explored in the next section, will lend the world some hope.

# SECTION FOUR

# REFORM AND CHANGE

# CHANGE FROM WITHIN

*Our attitude about change is one of the few things we can actually change.*

They say all real change begins within. It begins within us as individuals, and also within our families, our circles, our organizations. Meaningful change from outside tends to fail. For me, change (enlightenment?) was triggered by the infamous rhythm method of Catholic birth expansion—er, control. Four daughters in five years and an exhausted, health-threatened wife instigated my personal look within. Big families were in our family's religious DNA. My then- wife and I combined had eighteen siblings and we were on track to generate our own little population explosion. I am eternally grateful for my four extraordinarily charming and successful daughters and the families they formed. But when my youngest daughter was born, it felt in every way that our family was complete.

A need to swell the ranks of tiny Catholics started to seem like the logical explanation for the Church's prohibition of any modern birth control method likely to actually control births. The joke was, what do they call Catholic couples who practice the rhythm method? Answer: parents. Odd, but questioning the Church's motives on effective birth control started me wondering about all the other rules and regulations required to maintain good standing. Bad standing, of course, was not after-Mass detention but mortal sin and eternal damnation if you died in that state.

The quiet questioning process began slowly, given the years of accepting all moral matters on faith. The authority of the Church was not to be questioned, and for twenty-some years I had more or less complied. But in the late 1960s, surrounded by intelligent, well-meaning, and well- educated fellow Navy pilots, I discovered alternate points of view. My morals might not have been their morals. Their rules might have been different. Yet, they and their families seemed just as worthy as any

Catholic family I knew. Slowly the blinders came off. Slowly I became less judgmental, more tolerant of other religious and non-religious lifestyles.

The world revolved and evolved at its previous pace. The change was inside me.

Blessed with the opportunity to live in Japan and Okinawa and visit much of surrounding Asia, I met folks who didn't even know what a Catholic was. It dawned on me (duh!) that most of the world was non-Catholic and doing fine, thank you. My indoctrination mind-set was not easily dissuaded. These ubiquitous pagans needed to be converted, according the Church. Daily, that seemed more and more far-fetched to me. Serving in a very high-risk occupation led me to maintain my religious "insurance policy" for a couple more years. Then I cancelled and "went bare"; that is, without any spiritual insurance. I couldn't find a replacement policy. Perhaps my attitude made me spiritually uninsurable. I saw much the same as what I left in other denominations and very little meaningful reform anywhere.

Along the way there was war. For me, Vietnam. I always thought we in the United States were the good guys. Not having heard from any church source that this war (or any war) was immoral, I arrived on my white horse (okay, aluminum fighter jet) ready to defend democracy. Even in the absence of any Catholic or other organized-religion protest, I began to have doubts about the rightness of a non-defensive conflict so far from the homeland. I had chosen an unarmed Navy support squadron not in the business of dropping bombs. But still I felt part of the problem.

Change happened within me, as well, when I met Vietnamese face-to-face on their home ground and learned first hand they didn't really want us there. If we were there in error, where was the Christian objection? What purpose was worth the dislocation and destruction we were visiting on this tiny country? Reasons were given, such as the domino theory that warned what would befall us at the hands of godless Soviet communism and Chinese imperialism, should we concede a single country to them. I didn't understand: what was the role of religion if not to advise on so moral a matter as war? Yes, some religious forces did get involved, but that was after many secular minds and most young folks had already seen and protested our mistake.

Virtually all religions began with a call to treat our neighbors as we

would want to be treated. Conquest, domination, control, and subjugation were not the call of the prophets. Yet, despite pious protests to the contrary, much of religion wound up directly or indirectly in support of a secular sovereign. Its purity was corrupted.

In *The Varieties of Religious Experience*, William James observes the frequency with which religious geniuses [prophets] attract disciples, and produce groups of sympathizers. When these groups get strong enough to "organize" themselves, they become ecclesiastical institutions with corporate ambitions of their own. The spirit of politics and the lust of dogmatic rule are then apt to enter and to contaminate the originally innocent thing.

It seems corruption just naturally follows self-appointment to the role of righteous interpreter of all that is holy and sacred. The resulting need to sort through myriad, often self-serving, spiritual interpretations has handicapped the human race. This may explain why there have been so many prophets and why folks have been a little slow putting their simple, profound words into practice.

As a result of my studies, I have come to realize that the day after religions organized, reform movements began. Spiritual ideas have competed with one another from day one. Surrounded by all-knowing Catholicism, at first I didn't see the need for this competition or for reform. Now I see that no unchanged, monolithic organized religion exists. And this doesn't bother me. There are seven billion variations of religious and spiritual belief: one variation, however slight, for each person in the world today. Built into the very concept of religion is the challenge of reform. As times change, religion that seeks to survive must update and reform. And that change begins within individuals of courage and character.

Jews Micah and King Josiah, and later Zoroaster, opposed the corrupt prevailing religious views, advocated reform, and became understandably unpopular with the defensive priestly classes.

Buddha protested Vedic Hinduism and its privileged Brahmin class, Jesus the abuses of the Jewish rabbis and the Roman ruling class, Muhammad the tribal polytheism and selfish commercialism, Luther the abuses of the Roman Catholic hierarchy, and Baha'u'llah the abuses and intolerance of Islam.

Religion grows in a climate of social oppression. And religious reforms or new religions grow through religious oppression. The mainguy founder sets up basic neighborly principles; after he dies, his followers quickly transform the original ideas into self-serving ritual and dogma. In time, the new order becomes oppressive in social, economic, spiritual, or physical ways, and the seed is planted for a new spiritual crop.

Today the stage is set for quantum reform from within all organized religion—especially fundamentalist Christianity and fundamentalist Islam. Internal pressures are building for moderating (if not burying) the literalist point of view. There might be less than a full chorus at this point, but strong single voices are clamoring for change that reaches beyond merely condemning acts of terrorism and religious justifications for war.

Deepak Chopra describes it well in *Peace is the Way*: "If any religion would make the same choice to join the way of peace that individuals are making every day, faith would be a living force once again." And he says, "Religion must place the responsibility for violence squarely where it belongs, in the mind of every person. It must stop judging others outside the faith as sinners condemned by God."

New ways are forming to look at those encrusted religious beliefs and practices that so far have eluded the forces of reform over hundreds or even thousands of years. Perhaps this will be a time of historic reform. Even in the case of anachronistic organized world religions, the chipping away of protective creed by dissatisfied believers has begun to take place.

Bowing to its community's call for reform, Judaism allowed female rabbis only as recently as about forty years ago, and today nearly one thousand women have been ordained. Orthodox Jews have not yet accepted women as rabbis. Buddhism and Hinduism have made some efforts to open to new ideas and grow with the times. But critical, world-altering changes loom especially for the two largest faiths: Christianity and Islam.

Are they up to the task?

Large bureaucracies share a revulsion of meaningful change. Typically they are moved to action only when forced, only when they have no other option. They catch up and try to board the ship of change after it has set sail. Both Christianity and Islam are in danger of missing the boat upon which much of their membership has embarked.

# CHRISTIAN REFORM

*The longer things stay the same the more likely they are to change.*

Galileo and other great Catholic minds were branded heretics and infidels by the Catholic Church. Persecution clearly had a chilling effect on modernizing ideas. Even now, some Church conservatives long for the good old days of the Middle Ages, when everyone from the king down recognized that the Pope's word ruled.

Early Christian leaders declared themselves the one, true, and only path to salvation. They've labored ever since to prove their claim. If Christians were to be the new chosen people, these leaders thought, Jesus couldn't be just another prophet; he must be God. Since Father God already existed above the clouds in heaven, Jesus must be His Son. Then, surely, Jesus had been miraculously conceived in the womb of an immaculately conceived virgin. Add the Holy Spirit to complete the doctrine of the Trinity—a doctrine that is difficult to construct, explain, and defend. Yes, creating dogma and working outside the bounds of reason is complicated and demanding work.

For a human even to imagine the nature of God—with a Jewish Son, already—is like a hamster trying to imagine the nature of a human. Christians believe Jesus was God because he appeared truly amazing to them and because the Church declared it so. But could any mom or dad imagine a loving, compassionate God the Father who would condemn his Son Jesus to be crucified? Somehow this bloody sacrifice could atone for the evils of earlier generations (as in, let's have the children be responsible for the sins of their parents)? Yet the early Church needed a way to explain the Crucifixion of their hero. The doctrine of atonement resulted.

To ensure the survival of Christianity (and their clergy jobs?), early Church leaders claimed absolute infallibility interpreting "matters of faith and morals." They assumed sole authority to interpret the Bible, and in particular the meaning of the life and death of Jesus. Based on Jesus calling Peter a rock, and consistent with the divine rights of kings, they claimed the right to forever appoint their successor Popes.

Regardless of extravagant church claims, however, each generation has nonetheless redefined religion for itself. A characteristic of all major world religions surviving the centuries is they have slowly evolved to suit believers and the social times. Infallible or not, Christians (Catholics) today would not buy a new Pope-sanctioned Crusade or a Church- sponsored Inquisition.

Especially since Martin Luther nailed his gripes to the cathedral door, punting and drop-kicking Christian dogma has become a popular world sport. Many take to the field to challenge the Vatican home team.

The *National Catholic Reporter*, in a May 3, 2002 poll summary, suggests a hopeful glimmer of reform from within the Church. "Blueprint for Vatican III" polled priests, women, and religious- and lay- persons, mostly from emerging growth areas of Catholicism (especially Asia, Oceania, Africa, and Latin America/Mexico). The respondents included a Church cardinal from a developing country, three bishops, a woman missionary, and an Asian priest, among others. The object was to propose key agenda items for hoped-for major Catholic Church reform.

The cardinal suggested all religions be invited to a Vatican III Council, and that they be given voting rights. He advocated "the integration of the East and all its religions." Another said that the Church "must face the reality that religious pluralism is part of God's plan for humanity... and to understand Christianity as one of many [religions]... particularly with Islam and the religions in Asia."

Gender and racial justice, including the move away from "a celibate caste for ritual," was proposed for both spiritual and pragmatic reasons. Many respondents chafed at the centralized hierarchical management model focused on blind obedience, concluding "1,700 years of a Roman Empire-style governance is sufficient." It was suggested that worldly titles, such as Eminence, Excellency, and Holiness, be reconsidered and that "watered silk, lace blouses, billowing capes, little beanies, jeweled crosses and rings, etc., are counterproductive to the gospel values."

A respondent asked if it made sense that the "second largest denomination in the United States is un-churched Catholics," due mostly to "irregular marriages," and suggested it was time to reexamine rules about divorce.

Reform, though, moves in fits and starts. All of the key players are pedal to the metal; however, some have their foot on the accelerator and others on the brake.

The Vatican III concept of ecumenism and reconciliation might have to wait for the next Pope. Pope emeritus Benedict XVI considered Roman Catholics as the chosen ones and all other non-Catholics as deficient in faith and morals. The dream of reconciliation has evaporated for many, but some have hopes for Pope Francis.

There is ongoing pressure to reform the Anglican world (originally Church of England), and especially the Episcopal Church of the United States. The Episcopalians are an autonomous part of the Anglican Communion and follow similar worship and ministerial orders, but are more liberal.

Episcopalians introduced reforms in their liturgy, a new prayer book, and elected their first woman bishop, Barbara Harris. But their consecration of an openly gay man, Gene Robinson, as bishop of New Hampshire, caused major dissension within the Anglican Communion and with other anti-gay Christian denominations.

Then, in 2006, Bishop Katharine Jefferts Schori was elected Presiding Bishop of the Episcopal Church. The American congregations' choice has increased the possibility of a split with the world Anglican Communion, especially conservative members in Africa and developing countries. It is the classic battle of individual reformers against the corporate bureaucracy.

Thanks to modern polling, we now know what religious people believe to be important, and how they act on their beliefs. George Barna, author of *Revolution: Finding Vibrant Faith Beyond the Walls of Sanctuary*, has long been a prominent Christian pollster of the conservative evangelical type. He frequently offends conservative evangelical church leaders, though, by reporting what they do not want to hear. He points out, for example, that the divorce rate does not differ between born-again Christians and non- Christians, and that for the born-agains, God ranks behind "living a comfortable lifestyle." These Christians are changing their beliefs to suit the lives they lead.

Barna now touts a new Revolutionary Age and compares it to the time of the Apostles, the martyrs, and the Reformation. He stopped commercial polling, downsized his new Barna Group, and now supports "churchless Christians", who seem to be making as good or better progress in the good life as compared with their churched brethren.

Christian churches, however, are not advocating that people stop going to church. Rank and file reverends feel insulated against change by their bargaining unit, the Union of Concerned Clerics, which fights to protect their jobs. Nonetheless, Catholic bishops and leaders of the other Christian faiths are showing a few God-loving signs in their efforts to reach a pluralistic truce and a semblance of religious freedom for all.

Both liberals and conservatives agree the trend is away from the organizational church and toward the personal faith of the founder. Now-retired Episcopal Bishop John Shelby Spong promotes a Christianity of "love in our lives rather than judgment." The titles of Bishop Spong's books describe his efforts to reform his church from within. He authored *Rescuing the Bible from Fundamentalism*.

Supporters say Spong rejects the close-mindedness and fear and the stifling literal dogma advocated by fundamentalist Christians in the corporate church culture. In *Why Christianity Must Change or Die*, he challenges readers to look beyond the conditioning of traditional views. He arouses vitriol because he takes direct aim at the heart of fundamentalism:

Those who think that Christianity consists of a supernatural deity who invades the world periodically, who works through a virgin birth, a physical resuscitation, and a cosmic ascension, will find all that I say a threat to their faith. Those who believe that creeds are literally true, Bibles are inerrant, or popes are infallible will find me a challenge to their presuppositions. Those who have made the consensus of yesterday their only understanding of truth will call this heresy.

To respond to the familiar bumper sticker: *What would Jesus say* to the literal (Bible-thumping) fundamentalists of today? Probably the same thing he said to the Jewish (Torah-thumping) fundamentalists of his day: Get back to the real message—the Kingdom of God is within us, and is acknowledged by accepting Him and by showing justice and charity to our neighbors. Jesus was a little about the hereafter and a lot about the here on earth.

Thomas Sheehan, in *The First Coming,* says the kingdom Jesus introduced and celebrated was the immediate presence of God as a loving Father. This was a simple but radical protest against the legalistic, apocalyptic Jewish dogma of the day, and one guaranteed to offend the Jewish status quo. Sheehan describes Jesus' Father-God image as a personal presence and a personal call to justice, charity, and mercy, not an external kingdom and not a new religion at all. In fact, it was the end of religion as it was known then to the Pharisees. According to this view, Jesus, a fellow reform-minded Jew, preached a return to the basic truths of Judaism; that is, revere God by loving your neighbor.

We all know the unadulterated Jesus message is not easy to accept. Much personal comfort comes from belonging to the "in club" of corporate Christianity and having a heavenly Father to protect us. But most Christian reformers agree there are many clubs; that is, many doorways and pathways to understanding and accepting God.

Christianity will become embarrassingly irrelevant and eventually die if Christians maintain they alone are the light, the path, and the sole sanctioned way; that they (not the Jews) are now God's chosen ones. Based upon the legions of nominal Christians who didn't choose but were merely born into the family or community religion, radical change will be required for the survival of organized Christianity. Many Christians already live a spiritual life not sanctioned by their churches. Some just change their lives. Some hope to change their church. The ship of reform (and survival) is leaving the dock.

# MUSLIM REFORM

*Reform happens slowly when the price of trying may be dying.*

In spite of the severe personal and social costs of dissension in Islam, voices call out for reform from within the Muslim world. You won't hear much from Saudi Arabia, though, with its Islamist, Wahhabi-wack-'em method of stifling divergent ideas about Islam. But Saudi Arabia discovered recently that financing and condoning terrorism ultimately comes back home. Preaching destruction of infidels creates loose cannons. It bombs the hand that funds it.

One surprising reform voice comes from cleri-cratic, Islamist-led Iran. The 2003 Nobel Peace Prize winner, Shirin Ebadi, speaks her mind. This Muslim lawyer, judge, lecturer, writer, and activist speaks out for human rights, especially for women and children. In her Nobel lecture on December 10, 2003 she said,

> Some Muslims, under the pretext that democracy and human rights are not compatible with Islamic teachings and the traditional structure of Islamic societies, have justified despotic governments, and continue to do so…. The Koran [Qur'an] swears by the pen and what it writes. Such a sermon and message cannot be in conflict with awareness, knowledge, wisdom, freedom of opinion and expression and cultural pluralism.
> The discriminatory plight of women in Islamic states, too… has its roots in the patriarchal and male-dominated culture prevailing in these societies, not in Islam. This culture does not tolerate freedom and democracy… and the liberation of women from male domination… because it would threaten the historical and traditional position of the rulers and guardians of that culture.

Even a faint glimmer of reform flickers in Saudi Arabia, despite the long-running repressive Saudi/Wahhabi joint venture. King Abdullah, walking a religious/political tightrope, pardoned three liberal dissidents for their crime of petitioning for a written constitution. And without reprisal, leading Saudi cleric Sheikh al-'Abikan publicly stated that suicide terrorism is a crime against civilians, and that al Qaeda terrorism has been a catastrophe for world Muslims.

King Abdullah II of Jordan, a noted Muslim moderate, had this to say when marking the end of Ramadan in 2002:

> Our religion calls us to live and work for justice and to promote tolerance.... This is the true voice of Islam, but... Americans... hear the hatred spewed by groups mistakenly called Islamic fundamentalists. In fact... they are religious totalitarians, in a long line of extremists of various faiths who seek power by intimidation, violence and thuggery....
>
> The Prophet Muhammad tells us that the "greater" holy war [jihad] is not against others at all but against one's own failings— the "war against the ego...."
>
> So when today's terrorists target innocents, they provide direct evidence of their real agenda: power politics, not religion. In fact, long before so-called Islamic terrorists began attacking the West, they were targeting fellow Muslims. The goal was to silence opposition and obliterate the Islam of peace and dialogue....
>
> Among the world's 1.2 billion Muslims, extremists are... a tiny minority. For decades, many Muslims thought that because they had nothing to do with this criminal fringe, they could ignore it. Sept. 11, 2001, changed that kind of thinking. The idea that anyone would exploit our religion to sanction the killing of innocents outraged Muslims everywhere....
>
> Today Muslims must speak out boldly in defense of a dynamic, moderate Islam—an Islam that upholds the sanctity of human life, reaches out to the oppressed, respects men and women alike, and insists on the fellowship of all humankind. This is the true Islam of the Prophet, and the Islam that terrorists seek to destroy.

The recent Malaysian prime minister, Abdullah Ahmad Badawi, made a formal address to the August 2004 Faith and Order Commission of the World Council of Churches in Malaysia. He highlighted the need for dialogue between Christians and Muslims at a time when tensions between the two were escalating. Badawi said moderation was important, and pointed out that "many people [Islamic radicals] practice their faith in absolutist terms.... They refuse to take into account the modern world in which we live. They refuse to understand that so much of religious teaching is shaped by the context of the society in which it originated."

Even high-level Muslim clerics have begun to question previously unquestioned obedience and devotion to the Muslim hierarchy as interpreters of the Qur'an. Like the Bible, the Qur'an has begun to be scientifically studied in recent years and has been found historically wanting. Like the Bible, the Qur'an is now known to have been written primarily after the fact and in a manner to suit the times and the audience. An example is the misinterpretation during the past few decades by the extremists who talk of jihad.

Egypt's former top cleric, Al-Azhar Grand Imam, Sheikh Muhammad Sayyed Tantawi, who held the highest seat of learning in the Sunni Muslim world (and longest title?), denounced the London 2005 bombings, saying, "Those responsible for London attacks are criminals who do not represent Islam or even truly understand [its message]."

And renowned Egyptian scholar Sheikh Yusuf Al-Qaradawi, chairman of the International Association of Muslim Scholars, condemned the July 2005 terrorist attack on Sharm El-Sheikh, in his country, saying, "All divine religions in general and Islam in particular assert the sanctity of human life and strongly prohibit aggression against it." He emphasized that Islam considers the killing of other people as one of the gravest of sins in the sight of Allah, and stressed that such grisly incidents are prohibited by the Islamic Shari`ah: "Such heinous sin and abominable crime lead to Allah's curse in this world and His severe punishment in the Hereafter."

Though there are many radical opposing points of view, the moderate approach appears to be on the rise. In most Muslim countries, the typical Muslim is not well educated in matters of the faithful interpretation of the Qur'an. Some imam shopping goes on to find compatible and acceptable religious messages of guidance. The Qur'an doesn't discourage this. (Shopping for spiritual inspiration seems common to all religions.) So the moderate religious leaders of Islam in Muslim countries must lead from within the reformation toward a tolerant and peaceful coexistence of the Muslim world.

Some Muslims in the Western world, of course, also speak out. Souleiman Ghali, president of the Islamic Society of San Francisco, said he would never tolerate among his people the indoctrination of hatred or killing. Various national and international Muslim organizations have condemned the attacks on civilians, but action by these organizations seems limited.

Perhaps the most famous Western Muslim dissident is Salman Rushdie, of 1980s *The Satanic Verses* fame. What he wrote and the consequences of writing it are illustrative of the current condition of Islamic reform. Rushdie describes an atmosphere of clerical aggrandizement not unlike what Jesus confronted and Luther hoped to diminish. Rushdie paid the price for his dissidence with a condemning fatwa (religious edict) and a $2.8 million tag on his head. Perceived criticism of Muhammad, the Qur'an, an Ayatollah, mullah, imam, or any Muslim leader is not taken lightly.

Rushdie is a London novelist, not a religious scholar, who was born in India to a Muslim family. Today he advocates nothing less than an Islamic reformation. According to Middle East Online, he urged Muslims to see the Qur'an as a historical document and to reinterpret it to suit the new conditions of successive new ages. Rushdie states, "The insistence within Islam that the Koranic text is the infallible, uncreated word of God renders analytical scholarly discourse all but impossible. Why would God be influenced by the socioeconomics of seventh-century Arabia, after all?" After the July 7, 2005 attack that killed dozens in London's public transportation system, Britain's largest Sunni Muslim group issued a binding edict condemning the suicide attack, stating that the Qur'an forbade suicide attacks and that such terrorism is a sin that could send the perpetrators to hell.

In the United States, the British Muslims' anti-suicide fatwa was echoed by the Fiqh (Islamic legal issues) Council of North America and the Muslim Public Affairs Council, as well as the Council on American-Islamic Relations. Other faiths joined in. Rabbi David Saperstein, director of a Reform Judaism group and former member of the U.S. Commission on International Religious Freedom, agreed with the moderate Muslim position. He said, "Ultimately, it is Muslims who are going to need to win the battle about the direction and the future of Islam."

Former Democratic senator from Georgia, Sam Nunn, also sees Muslim moderates playing a key role: "The key long term, around the globe, on terrorism is mobilizing and helping Muslim communities to protect their own religion from the abuse it is receiving from the fundamentalists who believe in violence and... are using religion to make a very terrible conduct." He says it will take not planes, ships, and tanks to turn the moderates against the extremists, but rather a psychological battle.

Gilles Kepel, a French scholar of radical Islam, agrees, with a twist: "The most important battle in the war for Muslim minds... will be fought... on the outskirts of London, Paris, and other European cities, where Islam is already a growing part of the West." And so the reformation seems to be beginning around us.

The huge irony is that the destruction of the World Trade Center and the heinous terrorist activities around the world ultimately may lead to a full-fledged Islamic protest reformation and not the Islamist world envisioned by the perpetrators.

Although we have mostly come to terms with biblical biases within the Judeo-Christian tradition, it is sometimes difficult for Westerners to reconcile the inequality between men and women implied in the Qur'an. But Islamic mores have changed and moderated in some Muslim countries, such as Morocco and Algeria. These countries have instituted universal suffrage and limited abortion rights, and have somewhat reconciled gender inequalities. Recently, Chad and Uganda, two countries with a Muslim minority, have made efforts toward moderating gender bias. Women in Kuwait joined their sisters from Gulf neighbors Qatar, Oman, and Bahrain in gaining the vote. Women in Indonesia have been able to vote for half a century and now hold twenty percent of seats in the Regional Representatives Council (DPD, their Senate), a higher percentage than in the U.S. Senate.

We may think of current Islam as a joining of religion and politics, with religion dominating. But another possibility, even likelihood, is that politics and the governed will conversely affect the doctrines of Islam. The health and welfare of women, and thus nations, has and will continue to foster religious change.

Muslim countries that have attained levels of personal freedom are quite different than those stuck with totalitarian regimes. Compare relatively moderate Islam in Indonesia or in most of Malaysia with Islam in retrograde, fundamentalist Saudi Arabia. Where people are freer to think and act as they wish, religion becomes moderated and decidedly more liberal. Fundamentalists blame modern, Western-style free economies for steering Muslims away from the literal word of the Qur'an. But, more likely, increasing religious tolerance and healthier economies within the Arab world result from the granting (or claiming) of personal freedom.

It seems unlikely that literalism can survive long in an environment of individual freedoms. Even closed societies are influenced today by their free neighbors, who are all electronically in the same room. Geographic borders are routinely penetrated by bits and bytes of data chipping away at the unsustainable foundations of fundamentalism.

Islamic scholarship and independent study of the Qur'an are positioned roughly where Bible study was two hundred years ago— beginning to look at the historical facts of who wrote what, when, and why. Placing the Qur'an and other ancient writings into the perspective of mid-first-millennium society, and comparing their context with modern social conditions, now seem inevitable. The literalist fight to preserve thus becomes rear-guard action battling the massive army of history.

Outside help and alliances, however, may be unwise and unwanted. Moderate Muslims need to change from within their own communities and bless themselves with the personal and public courage to act on their beliefs. If it is true that Islamo-terrorists are a tiny percentage of the Muslim world, then the majority must step up and rescue their blessed Islam from the destructive extremists' violence.

I'm not an expert, but my reading of the Qur'an suggests a powerful, poetic message of tribal reform, peace, tolerance (of some), and compassion (along with some practical advice for 630 CE survival). The literal translation of *Islam* is "submission to Allah," and *Qur'an* means "to recite." These don't sound like fighting words. If the masses of moderate Muslims also see it this way, they would be well served to quickly board their own ship of reform already setting sail. Best not to wait for the Islamic clerical leadership, who—like most Christian clergy—will be left behind in port.

# ONE OR MANY?

*What will religion be—a force of domination or of tolerance and acceptance?*

The institutional religious impulse is to dominate. The two most populous and powerful religions—Christianity and Islam—have fought for supremacy since soon after their inceptions. Today each seeks to be the one-and-only world religion. Ever since St. Paul followed Jesus and the caliphs followed Muhammad, these religions have, as a matter of policy, each sought to convert the world. At the leadership level, neither believes there is room for more than one true religion. This is the concept of religious **monopoly**.

The greatest sin of organized religion must be pride (in the form of lack of humility and barely disguised arrogance). This leads adherents of a religion to believe their leaders and loyal followers speak for God. Or worse—that *only their religion* speaks for God. Jesus preached and practiced acceptance and love. Muhammad taught acceptance (at least of other Peoples of the Book) and tolerance for others. What hath God wrought through the followers of His prophets? How did revelations of two holy men result in disciples so exclusionary and hostile to all but their own devotees?

The world's religions are essentially just different roads leading to the same place. There is nothing monopolistic at their roots. But you surely wouldn't know it by watching the extraordinary ways they've marked off their territory with elaborate services, practices, rituals, and prayers. Muslim, Buddhist, Hindu, Jew, or Christian—each group insists its own variations are crucial, exclusive, meaningful, and even essential to its faith.

Friendly competition and the richness and variety of religions, cultures, and people do make this earth an interesting and rewarding place. But can we at least appreciate and respect other points of view? The perspective of **pluralism** (many, not just one) holds that no religion has an exclusive monopoly on the truth. This pluralistic view fosters public

117

tolerance—and ideally, acceptance and respect—for others' religions and perspectives. It downplays differences in ritual and practice and plays up common beliefs, such as the existence of one God, loving your neighbor, and living a virtuous lifestyle. Pluralism means simply being friends and good neighbors with believers of different faiths or of no faith at all.

However, in all of recorded history, seldom have religions seen eye to eye. Rather, it's been an eye *for* an eye. Faiths clash when they confuse basic beliefs with practice or ritual, or when they fantasize that only their religion can be true. They lose all sight of the fact that their belief lies in the realm of interpretation and is merely used as the language of their community. And that other interpretations also can be valid.

Given the survival instincts of corporate religion, no clerical leadership is likely to announce that its church is no more than one of many. Embedded in the lure of monopoly and job security are the very human traits of denial and self-protection. Yet this insistence that only we are the chosen ones and the rest of you are going to hell is a one-way ticket to the discord and war we've seen for two millennia. An attitude of pluralism needs to come from the rank and file and courageous individuals. It won't come from the hierarchy.

If scripture, laws, and doctrines are seen literally and exclusively, conflict is inevitable. According to liberal author Marcus Borg, "Protestants have rejected the Catholic Church's claim to have a monopoly on salvation. But they have nevertheless most commonly claimed a Christian monopoly: 'Salvation is only through Jesus, and we've got Jesus.'" And he concludes, "When Christianity claims to be the only true religion, it loses much of its credibility."

The opposite of a monopoly is the all-of-the-above approach, which accepts expansive beliefs in everything and particular beliefs in nothing. This perspective can be described as pluralism on double espresso. An example is seen in text from the Unitarian Universalist Association of San Francisco website:

> *Welcome to Our Community!*
> *Sunday Worship Service at 11 am every Sunday*
> *Since 1850 Unitarian Universalists have been a prophetic and progressive voice within the city. Our church is a place where individuals are free to*

*explore the ultimate questions in a community of other seekers and find their own answers.*

*We are...*

- *Christians, Jews, Humanists, Agnostics, Pagans, Buddhists, Taoists, Hindus, Muslims, and many other faith traditions*
- *straight, gay, couples, singles, young, and old*
- *bound together not by dogma, but by shared values, social concerns, common interests, and friendship.*

Like the Unitarians, people in many societies today get along quite nicely in an atmosphere of diversity and freedom of beliefs and practices. Religion seems to thrive in these places where it is a matter of personal choice. The United States and many Western countries are examples of such societies.

However, some state-religion models, such as those in Singapore and Indonesia, also function in a relatively tolerant way. What I saw on a visit to Malaysia on September 11, 2002 confirmed a friendly and pluralistic culture. Except in two northeast fundamentalist provinces, citizens displayed cordial attitudes toward Westerners, Chinese, and Indians— much like in nearby friendly (if-you-follow-the-rules) Singapore. The economy and personal activity seemed relatively accepting of a diverse mix of religious beliefs. Yet Malaysia is an officially Muslim country. In Kuala Lumpur, although the Rotary club was still all male, women generally wore modern dress and were seen everywhere. Fully- veiled tourist women from Saudi Arabia were accepted and not singled out. Within officially Muslim Indonesia, Bali, for example, is Hindu, and various areas house Buddhist and other religious enclaves. All this is progressively pluralistic and a sharp contrast to the Wahhabi repression reported in Muslim-or-else Saudi Arabia and cleric-ruled Iran.

Nevertheless, pluralism and tolerance do not necessarily mean unchecked religious freedom. All countries restrict religion according to generally accepted standards of public morality. For example, polygamy was once permitted by Mormons but is outlawed by the U.S. government. However, per Reza Aslan, "The Qur'an does not allow any religion [or presumably government] to violate core Muslim values." But also in the Qur'an: "There can be no compulsion in religion." In other words, as a moderate Muslim, I am instructed to accept or at least tolerate your beliefs, but don't ask us Muslims to violate ours.

Diana Eck, author of *A New Religious America*, notes that here "tolerance [is less than acceptance and] comes from a position of strength." She points out it is easy for us to tolerate minority points of view when we're the ones in power, but asks what this means for those who are members of the minority. For the minority, tolerance may be experienced as less than fair and equal. For example, Catholics officially tolerate Protestant sects, yet believe their doctrine is inferior and don't fully accept them into the family of faith because they don't support papal authority. Similarly, Muslim majorities tolerate Jews and Christians, but don't accept them as equal to their own. Eck concludes, "Tolerance can create a climate of restraint, but not a climate of understanding."

An inherent danger of monopolistic religion is that it is almost always intolerant and usually joined at the hip to politics. Both Islam and Christianity have been inexorably tied to national and international politics, especially to the external politics of assuring world dominance of their brand of faith.

Moses, Jesus, and Muhammad were all politicians challenging the political/religious monopoly of their day. Stand back while lightning strikes the blasphemy. But all major religions were, in fact, born out of a challenge to an existing political order—typically, an oppressive, unfair, and exclusionary political regime tied to a religious status quo: Moses versus the Pharaoh and his favorite gods; Jesus versus the corrupt, ritual-bound Pharisees; Muhammad versus moneyed Meccans and desert tribe-enforced religious traditions.

Since the beginning of religion and politics, both have used each other in good and bad ways. For the case of the good side, consider this: Christianity might have fizzled if Constantine I, in the fourth century, hadn't made Christianity legal, and if Theodosius I hadn't made it the state religion of the Roman Empire. This partnership, though, was not born in heaven. The bad side was when mama's-boy Constantine got the blessing of his converted Catholic mother, Helena, by putting the kibosh on Arian (Jesus ain't equal to God the Father) heresy. Catholics gained a patron as well as legal status. Theodosius went on to smite the pagan competition and so-called Christian heresies. Acceptance and tolerance fell victim to a new religious monopoly.

Many other organized religions—certainly Islam and certainly Protestantism—got a political boost along the way. Some would argue that politically favored religions were helped but ultimately co-opted by governments. Nominal membership increased whenever a religion became a state command performance. But at what price to tolerance and pluralism?

Governments in countries with a religious monopoly have consistently used that religion to sanctify their rule. In many cases, they have used it to dominate the weak or helpless. Using God and religion for political purposes is a time-honored tradition, especially in the conduct of war and acquiring real estate. Two modern examples are the Wahhabi/Saudi and the Ayatollah/Iran cooperatives.

Religion has been unquestionably useful in countless battles and wars throughout history. Political leaders rarely are able to get ordinary, moral, just, and loving human beings to kill and maim other ordinary, moral, just, and loving human beings without invoking God to support their cause. God's work as justification is typically claimed by political leaders on both sides. The sense of working or fighting for God and the principles of right can be highly satisfying and motivating. Even more satisfying is claiming that the enemy is wrong and is doing the work of the devil. There have, however, been some legitimate benefits over the centuries, such as rallying citizens against the evil acts of the Axis powers during WW II (but do the ends justify the means?)

President Abraham Lincoln was one of the notable few in a position of great political power (in a pluralistic *Christian* society) to not co-opt religion to the political agenda and to humbly express doubt about just where God stood. During the U.S. Civil War, Lincoln wrote, "The will of God prevails. In great contests each party claims to act in accordance with the will of God. Both may be, and one must be wrong. God cannot be for and against the same thing at the same time." Lincoln pointed out that God could have either saved or destroyed the Union without a war at all. But Lincoln's thoughts were not widely shared. Many on both sides continued to believe God was only and surely on their side.

Leaders throughout history have found it simpler and more practical not to allow multiple religious groups, but rather convince a single clergy and buy them off with the state franchise. That is not an option in pluralistic societies in which religious and personal freedoms reign.

Not only have we avoided a monopolistic state religion, we've attempted to build a wall between politics and pluralistic religion in the United States, to keep each from controlling the other. Most other Christian societies and some Muslim countries have attempted similar separations. Overall, this separation has met with some success. But people are people, and it is important for many that others believe what they themselves believe. We talk about separation of church and state, but have these two ever really been totally separate—in the United States, the Western world, or anywhere in the world?

Modern religions have followers who argue the primacy of their beliefs and for religious freedom because they want to be able to practice without restrictions. But many of these same individuals would gladly give up *others'* religious freedom to see their own religion become the official government religion. To them, the separation of church and state is readily dispensable.

The United States could have had a single state religion. Had the Puritans or Anglicans gotten the upper hand, we would have been officially a Christian or perhaps a Puritan or Anglican nation. Before the states were united under the Constitution, Anglican state religions were established in Maryland, Delaware, North and South Carolina, and Virginia. Congregational state religions were established in Massachusetts, New Hampshire, and Connecticut.

Our Declaration of Independence declares that our Creator endowed "inalienable rights." From the very beginnings, religion in the United States was involved in the political process. In crafting our Constitution, the founders and religious leaders—who, as I mentioned earlier, tended to be wary of, if not hostile toward, organized religion— balanced freedom *from* religion with freedom *for* religion. The presence of multiple and competing religions may have accounted for the success of this strategy. And the resulting pluralistic, competitive religious society may in part account for the success of the United States as a country.

Does religion need to evolve to a pluralistic point to enable individual freedoms? Or is it the other way around? Are democracy and political freedoms preconditions for tolerant religion?

Some present-day political tyrannies grant no individual rights of speech or association, and certainly no freedom of religion. Captive citizens are allowed to practice only the state religion, be it Islam or (in the recent past) Communist atheism, or whatever. But today free men and women outside of captive societies can and are asking questions and demanding reform.

No tyranny is an island. Ideas of free people abroad now infiltrate formerly sealed societies, thanks to the Internet. So, North Korea and Saudi Arabia may not be ready for religious reform, but much of the rest of the world appears ready to assist the spiritually (and physically) oppressed, regardless of where they live. Has there ever been a society that has managed to forever stamp out either religious or individual freedoms? Has any society ever successfully forced on its people a lasting conversion to state religion?

Because of abuses observed in different countries over the centuries, people today worry: can religions be political without subverting the principles of either religious or political freedom? How do we prevent organized religions from pursuing evil political ends? How do we prevent politics from using religions for partisan or selfish political ends? Perhaps the potential (and rich history) of abuse on both sides is all the more reason for legitimate religions and genuinely spiritual people to be involved in politics and demand pluralistic policies, and for politicians to respect and practice the multiple moral and spiritual lessons of the founders of the great world religions.

Jim Wallis, activist evangelical preacher and author of *God's Politics*, thinks Christians (and others) should politically focus on the poor and dispossessed through their religions. He notes that "we have been buffeted by private spiritualities that have no connection to public life and a secular politics showing disdain for religion or even spiritual concerns. That leaves spirituality without social consequences and politics with no soul."

Monopolistic, corporate religion has always been tied to politics, but not usually in a good way. There is another way—the way of the many. The politics of freedom rests on the (often disregarded) principles of the world's many great religions: respect and dignity as an individual, inalienable, God-given right. Whether freedom of religions (plural) sets the stage for political freedom or political freedom allows for religious freedom, tolerance and acceptance are essential.

Let's accept personal responsibility for advocating pluralism and acceptance of others' spiritual beliefs. Can we be the practitioners and leaders of the next generation of religious reforms? This responsibility will be found not only in words, no matter how profound. It will be found in the present-day (the HERE) actions of ordinary individuals and courageous political and religious leaders. As Mahatma Gandhi so aptly said, "We need to be the change we wish to see in the world."

# ACTIONS SPEAK LOUDER THAN DOGMA

*What you do speaks louder than what you say.*—*Ralph Waldo Emerson*

What should we ask of world religions? And what do we get from them now? Many think institutional religion fails in filling their personal needs.

Multitudes have acted on their preferences and registered their disappointments by voting with their feet. They've walked away from church, temple, and mosque. They may say they believe in their born-into religion but have abandoned its practice. Many traditional congregations are looking gray, bald, or both. Consider that remaining older congregants have fifty or more years invested in their particular brand of salvation and aren't about to cash out their lifetime spiritual savings account. Many of the young (and not so young) have disappeared through the exits and entered the world church without doors or hallowed halls.

When you hear church alumni say, "I'm spiritual but not big on religion," they may mean "I'd rather have faith in football or soccer on Sunday or the Sabbath than trek to church/temple/mosque." It could mean "I was born into my family's religion, which no longer is relevant to me, so I've dropped out." Admirably, it could mean "I have examined my faith and other faiths carefully and decided to act in a compassionate and loving way without the benefit of organized religion."

We lead busy lives with family, kids, and work. We eat to gain weight, exercise to lose weight, and catch a little entertainment here and there. Who thinks that's going to change?

Most of us seriously want a more peaceful, just, and compassionate world. We know life on this planet is not fair. We know instinctively, morally, and practically that a reasonable standard of living for everyone means more security and happiness for all. But can we even conceive of a little more heaven on earth? A little more HERE and a little less hereafter?

We're put off by the enormity of the challenge. What can I do for the hundreds of millions who are oppressed and hungry—for food, freedom, and faith? Perhaps it is beyond us to eliminate all suffering. But how do we at least make life on the planet more fair?

Many of us do an admirable job of "feeding a person for a day." We have trouble getting our arms around "teaching that person to fish." Billions of dollars flow to organized religions and charities each year. Yet our progress in relieving hunger, injustice, and inequality is painfully slow and inadequate. We don't seem to be leveraging our money or our effort. Many religious and charitable resources are ground up in the process, with no meaningful or measurable change for the better. We're always behind the power curve and reacting to disasters. Considering all our noble and well-intentioned efforts throughout history, we sure still have a lot of poor people!

Our giving to help others can be leveraged into high-performance philanthropy through what I call the *control tab factor*. Pilots use control tabs to overcome opposing aerodynamic forces. Pilots get high-leverage help by manipulating little flaps on a plane's wings and tail. Those little tabs use aerodynamic leverage to overcome the great resistance of the high speed air. This same leverage concept can help us help others become self-sufficient.

For example, passing out twenty dollar bills to the homeless is a valuable means of feeding a person for a day. But politically contributing to a policy of fair-trade commodity prices for coffee and sugar imports from developing countries is an example of control tab leverage. It is like teaching a person to fish.

So what is going to work spiritually? How can we move beyond the dogma and ritual of our organized religion and its promises of next- life rewards and get control tab leverage on pressing here-and-now social issues of the twenty-first century? Each of us is likely to do it our way, inside or outside of religion. Consider some examples.

Justine Willis Toms, to keep from being overcome by the enormity of the task, does some HERE-things every day:

> I call my congressperson, I write a letter, I sign a petition, I educate myself, I have a conversation, I take a walk in nature, I lie in my

hammock. Each day I do at least one action that will contribute to a better world for all.

And she focuses on gratitude. If gratitude were a pill, she says, it would be a miracle drug.

Friend and co-worker Bob says Judaism is community. He compares his congregation to extended family and friends. Bob says religion creates a closeness beyond neighborliness, and speculates that historically it was "stick together in the desert, or die." He helps in his community and is a serious family man.

Daughter Jennifer says she isn't a Buddhist, but rather she and her family *practice* (Western) Buddhism. In other words, she and her family don't identify with an organized religious belief. They are just people who study, explore, and emulate the ways of a peaceful and learned man.

She finds more a sense of spiritual than social belonging through this practice; it gives her a belief system that is highly individualistic. Raised a Catholic, she chafed under the organizational monolith of the church and resented its judgmental atmosphere. She likes that Buddhism is less organizational and offers more of an explore-for-yourself approach. She also appreciates the philosophical advice not to maximize material possessions.

And unlike the Christianity with which she grew up, she says, "It never feels like I'm doing something wrong." In addition to her own personal growth, she (only half jokingly) feels it is "important my children have something to rebel against when they get older." More seriously, she wants to provide her children with "core or foundational values" and "a reality check about what is right and wrong."

So how are she and her husband to be judged? They lead a peaceful and kind and generous life. They are devoted to their family and are supporters of their community. They believe in a Greater Power, but they don't pass the ritual tests of Christianity, Islam, Hinduism, Baha'i, Judaism, or even of Buddhism.

My brother Paul actually studied to become a Roman Catholic Brother of the Viatorian Order. During a teaching apprenticeship, he studied and taught comparative world religions to high school seniors. To the eternal chagrin of our devout Catholic parents, he switched from Catholic to Baha'i, finding there a message that more closely fit his soul.

Paul is just as devout a Baha'i as he was a Christian. He became an expert in the teaching and doctrine of his new faith. Paul and his family "walked the talk"; that is, they lived their lives according to the principles of their faith. He and his then-wife served a two-year stint as missionaries in Brazil, where the first of two sons was born. Paul served as an activist and lobbyist in Washington, helping to protect Baha'is in Iran against religious persecution, and now is active in Texas.

Why is Paul a Baha'i? He sees religion as a way to "tie mankind's individual hearts back to their Creator." Why is this valuable? He says, "To give meaning to this crazy and beautiful world; to give purpose to life; to acquire virtue; and per Baha'u'llah (the founding key dude), to advance civilization."

Paul also talks about a "bigger plan here on earth"—one we learn about through "individual search, validation experiences, innate intellect [and] human history." He notes that the objective observer (and his brother Tom) will find a "series of spiritual teachers speaking with one voice, building on each other: Moses, Buddha, Krishna, Zoroaster, Jesus, Muhammad, the Báb and Baha'u'llah."

Sister Joni is a kind, generous-to-a-fault, loving person. She and her husband John share their musical talents by giving gratis concerts for deserving causes. Although Joni was raised a Catholic, she thinks structured religion is "pretty bogus," and that it was designed to suit the masses because they cannot figure it out on their own.

But she sees the value of organized religion for many people because "guilt is a powerful tool" to get them to behave. Joan cites the example of her Midwestern neighbors: their family saw a son's early death as punishment for going against religious teachings when they decided against having more children.

Although some attribute natural disasters to a vengeful God, Joni sees such events as "nature house cleaning," having nothing to do with peoples' behavior. She believes in a "gracious and loving God," but thinks questioning the nature of God in (any) organized religion would result in the questioner being "damned to hell."

And living solo in Florida was hundred-year old Aunt Helen. It's a wonder she hadn't been expelled or excommunicated because she sang in the choir and volunteered for church functions in both the Roman Catholic and Greek Orthodox churches, and had done so for more than fifty years. She stayed in good graces with both because she was too valuable a parishioner to be criticized by either church. She believed the centuries-old Eastern/Western schism had gone on quite long enough and hoped to see rapprochement before she died. Despite her best efforts that was not to be.

Aunt Henrietta (Auntie Retta, as we call her) approaching one hundred is Helen's younger sister. She lives in assisted living in Wisconsin. She believes and trusts in her Catholic faith in spite of being orphaned as a teenager, abandoned by a stepfather, nearly losing her son in an accident, and being widowed twice. Organized religion clearly works for this positive and upbeat human being. Until just a few years ago she spent much of her time volunteering in a Catholic hospice, working with "old folks." When questioned, she admitted that almost all of her clients then were younger than she was, but that they "needed my hugs." Besides, she says, they all brought enormous joy and purpose to her life.

My former brother-in-law is also a devout Catholic. He even teaches public school religion (PSR) because he believes "kids need a structure" and it's "important to belong to something—important for the family." He is not what he calls evangelical. He feels that it isn't only about "worshiping one true God"—everyone is entitled to his or her own belief. And it's okay for others not to believe at all. Still, he thinks the non-religious miss a kind of "enrichment."

What does he get out of his religion? The network of a local men's group, and having the security of knowing "the congregation is there for you in time of need."

In a sense of utter simplicity, Jesus directed us to love God with our whole heart, and similarly to love our neighbor. When we look at his life, there is no doubt he didn't just mean our affluent next-door neighbor. He especially meant those down-and-out prostitutes, prisoners, and generally yucky people. Grasping clean hands and wishing "God be with you" in church is good but not so difficult. Jesus was talking about difficult.

But God bless those who practice and live their faith in their organized religion. They actively promote compassion and justice, certainly within their religious community. World religions are built around these goals. But practice doesn't always reconcile with theory. And loving your family and friends and fellow worshipers turns out to be a lot easier than loving your cranky neighbor or your foreign "neighbor."

Muhammad said charity and compassion toward the poor were our basic, essential, and most important duties. He, too, focused on the especially vulnerable: the widows and orphans and those in need. Is there a major world religion that does not call for active justice and compassion as the will of God and make it our obligation to lead a good life?

So, just how much dogma do we need in our lives?

Do the anti-dogmas, "fallen-aways," renegades and religious quitters ask: Was Jesus God? How do we explain the Trinity? Was Muhammad the final prophet? Is the Bible or the Qur'an the final word? Are the Jews God's chosen people?

No, they don't seem to care.

They recognize those questions only make sense if you are trying to defend the One True Way of religious orthodoxy. Those questions matter only when trying to establish or prove a Chosen Faith. And fallen- aways generally don't see a need to embrace one true religion.

Perhaps the message of the great prophets was too simple to be able to successfully build an organized religion on it. Perhaps the message was thought too demanding to act out in everyday life, and so dogma, ceremony, and ritual became alternatives. Or perhaps generally illiterate humans at that time needed more structure and help. Perhaps some humans just thought they were more equal and better informed, better educated, closer to the source. And so they anointed themselves keepers of the Truth, channelers of the message.

Today many folks ask if we need interpreters, mediums, or filters for what was quite a simple message of love. Certainly there are benefits to the community of the faithful: educational, social, psychological, and physical support in each religious community.

According to Abraham Maslow, in *Religion, Values, and Peak-Experiences,*

Very many people in our [1960s] society apparently see organized religion as... the source, the custodian and guardian and teacher of the spiritual life. Its methods, its style of teaching, its content are widely and officially accepted as the path, by many as the only path, to the life of righteousness, of purity and virtue, of justice and goodness.

But it seems the organizational structure and beliefs—for example, Jesus was God and part of a Trinity—mostly serve to make Christianity exclusive. If Jesus was God, then how could any other religious belief compete? If Jesus was God, then Christianity must be the One True Religion for all times. Is that what Jesus—man or God—intended? Did he ever say, "I want to start the one true faith, to the exclusion of all others?" Or did he ever once say, "Let's see if we can replicate the hypocritical dogma and ritual I railed against to the Jewish rabbis?"

By incorporating the Jewish and Christian prophets and declaring Muhammad the last prophet, Islam created a similarly exclusive franchise. How can there be another religion or a refinement to the message of Allah? Is this what Muhammad intended in the Qur'an?

Growing up as a Catholic, missing Mass on Sunday was a mortal sin because (and I believed this) dying without confession meant going to hell. Eating meat on Friday was a serious offense. Divorce meant exclusion from the rites of the church and prohibition from marrying again.

Do we suppose Jesus cared what we ate on Fridays or on any other day?

What about a divorced man who never goes to Mass, eats meat every Friday, believes the Pope makes mistakes in faith and morals? But this man is kind, generous, loving, and spiritual in the best sense of the word. He turns the other cheek when insulted. He works hard and gives much to charity. Would he meet the ideal expressed by Jesus?

Good friend John Kelly, a fallen-away Catholic priest, officiated at the wedding of two fallen-aways: my then wife and me. John began priest training "right out of the eighth grade for the next twelve years." He served two years as parish priest, taught high school for fifteen years, and generally succeeded in teaching and other duties during his twenty-five years as a priest in good standing. But, in the early Seventies, he was called to greater social activism than the official church permitted: he joined a lay-person/priest racial segregation protest. John tells of the Jesus biblical message of the anti-racist Good Samaritan.

John, with a Notre Dame Masters in Theology, personally thinks that "Jesus' message does not necessarily jibe with [Church] officialdom, that Jesus was for justice for all fellow humans." He says, "Whether Jesus Christ was the only son of God is unimportant." John thinks the organizational church would be better served to "stop their obsession with sex, and focus on justice."

John directed his social activist energies to building a very successful community-based organization that annually provides 135,000 free meals for folks in need—no questions asked. Samaritan House is now in other capable hands and provides free health and dental clinics, no- charge clothing, and housing supplies. It generously serves the very same down-and-out people Jesus and Muhammad would have served and teaches them to fish, as well.

Retired John Kelly, age eighty-four, now serves as a volunteer at the hard-core state prison, San Quentin. He does it because, he says, "I find more spiritually there than in other places." John says he works with a nucleus of lifers, mostly murderers. He says now they have "a choice— to vegetate and rot, or decide 'I am somebody and I can still do some good.'" John jointly conducts sessions on Tuesday nights where he says prisoners recognize and identify with "awareness." John works particularly "to see that the young prisoners don't come back."

Abdul, a successful Silicon Valley software engineer and devout Muslim, does not get hung up on dogma. He says, "I'm Muslim, as true as I can be, because so many others who call themselves Muslim are not." Although a devoted husband and father, Abdul says, "I don't want to preach—even to my own three children. These kids are very intelligent.

They may come to a different and better conclusion regarding their beliefs."

Abdul reads the Qur'an every day, believes in the "basic and simple message of Islam," and is "open to others with different beliefs." He takes the environment very seriously, saying, "Humans are different than all other creatures and are God's trustees of this earth."

How about another Muslim who similarly leads a good life? She supports her community in charitable ways. She studies and works and supports her family with loving care. But she does not wear a veil and she drives a car. Would the God of Muhammad disapprove? Is she less deserving in the eyes of the most-merciful Allah? Perhaps certain rules of Islam were designed to serve other purposes (read: dogmatic control) and do not relate to the essence of the Islam faith.

The same arguments apply to any organized religion with rules and rituals beyond its basic message. Humans may need guidance and reminders of the main message. They may need help in the sense of their religious community. And it seems inarguable that organized religion does work for billions of people.

So, how do we reconcile institutional and mostly dogmatic world religions, which have worked for billions over two millennia, with modern society? One good possibility is through realizing that God exists in all of us humans, and maybe we really do need help in seeing and feeling God's presence. Maybe we need regular reminders, encouragement, and community. But do we need the dogma, the rules, or the rituals?

According to Abraham Maslow, "It is easier to be 'pure' outside an organization, whether religious, political, economic, or, for that matter, scientific. And yet we cannot do without organizations. Perhaps one day we shall invent organizations that do not 'freeze.'"

Back during the Enlightenment, the embodiment of the movement, Voltaire, proposed the ideal religion:

> Would it not be that which taught much morality and very little dogma? that which tended to make men just without making them absurd? that which did not order one to believe in things that are impossible, contradictory, injurious to divinity, and pernicious to mankind, and which dared not menace with eternal punishment anyone possessing common sense? Would it not be that which did not uphold its belief with executioners, and did not inundate the earth with blood on account of unintelligible sophisms? ... which taught only the worship of one god, justice, tolerance and humanity?

The Enlightenment philosophers maintained their belief in God, and Voltaire suggested that if God did not exist, it would have been necessary to invent him. "But," he said, "all nature cries aloud that he does exist: that there is a supreme intelligence, an immense power, an admirable order, and everything teaches us our own dependence on it."

What if a new religion were to start today? Maybe a Jewish/Christian/Muslim version would begin with a revised "Our Father":

> Our Father and Mother who art in Heaven in each of our hearts, Hallowed be Thy name, Thy Kingdom come, Thy Will be done on earth as it is in Heaven. Give us this day our daily bread and forgive us our trespasses as we forgive our brothers and sisters who trespass against us. Let us choose not be tempted by evil but to act with forgiveness, compassion, social justice, and love toward all beings in our earthly environment. Amen.

And as presumptuous as revising the Our Father may seem, religion in every age has adapted to the times. It must in order to survive.

I'd bet that a religion begun today would be light on dogma but uphold belief in one universal God. That God would be personal or mystical, in contrast with the distant, out-of-this world, disconnected Supreme Being of Aristotle and the philosophers.

Again Maslow : "Any religion, liberal or orthodox, theistic or non-theistic, must be not only intellectually credible and morally worthy of respect, but it must also be emotionally satisfying."

We need a God whom we can actually imagine. Some will be offended by the implication that God is of our imaginations, but I believe we need a God we can envision in ourselves and in our world neighbors. My guess is we would not need to imagine a three-person God whose son was born of a virgin.

As early as the twelfth century, the Iranian Yahya al-Suhrawardi (Sheikh al-Ishraq) attempted to connect all the religious insights of the world into a single, spiritual religion using imagination. He was ahead of his time and died in disgrace.

The danger is that a personal God we imagine could become not only an extension of the good, but also the evil within ourselves. God could then be a fundamentalist, a socialist, or a Republican, who knows? This could get thorny. Nevertheless, we do need a God who is not just an abstraction.

Deepak Chopra, in *How to Know God,* describes how to avoid the danger inherent in an imagined God:

> Every divine image remains an image; every vision tempts us to hold on to it. To be really free, there is no option except to be yourself. You are the living center around which every event happens, yet no event is so important that you willingly give yourself up to it.

We mostly need a God who is *useful* to humankind in the twenty-first century. A God who satisfies the human needs that fostered religions over the millennia. Religions—plural. Based on painful history, it seems exceedingly unlikely a single religion or a single concept of God will satisfy all world cultures now or ever.

Ibn al-Arabi, a Sunni Muslim, while on a Hajj back in 1201, had a vision convincing him we need more than rational arguments for us to love Allah (God). He said nothing could resemble Allah, so it would be difficult to love what amounted to an alien God. But, he concluded, we can love God's creatures: "If you love a being for his beauty, you love none other than God, for he is the Beautiful Being." And he said,

> Do not attach yourself to any particular creed exclusively, so that you may disbelieve all the rest; otherwise you will lose much good, nay, you will fail to recognize the real truth of the matter. God, the omnipresent and omnipotent is not limited by any one creed, for, he says, "Wheresoever ye turn, there is the face of al-Lah" (Qur'an 2:109).

There are 34,000 to 37,000 Christian groups alone and many different Muslim, Jewish, Hindu, and Buddhist groups, and hosts of other beliefs and practices. They continue to subdivide right now. We seem to be gravitating toward a de facto belief in a personal God, with every human having his or her own version of an Almighty.

The Internet and the World Wide Web today are what the printing press was to fifteenth century Europe. WebMD, Wikipedia, Google, Firefox, MS Explorer; are all names that open the world of information to everyone with a computer and online access.

In the Middle Ages, illiterate populations had to rely on clergy for knowledge of the world around them, especially because-we-said-so dogma. The Torah, Bible, and Qur'an were typically read by the rabbi, priest, or imam to an illiterate audience. Later, the general availability of printed books and increased literacy created direct information access. Martin Luther would have been no more than a historical footnote had he initiated his church reform a hundred years earlier, before the widespread printing of flyers, periodicals, and books.

Today the Internet and communication technology have created a quantum change in how people get information. National news is no longer the captured market of ABC, NBC, CBS, and the BBC. Now cable TV, blogs, specialty magazines, talk radio, and podcasts provide nearly unlimited sources for accessing information.

Is religion moving toward the proprietary Microsoft classic-church model, or the Linux anybody-can-contribute model? Will nobody or everybody own it? Will it use open or closed architecture; will its technology be interactive and compatible? Or perhaps it will adopt the Wikipedia model, in which the faithful contribute? Will it have a generally acknowledged scripture? Will it be free and democratic?

I've been thinking about these questions, and a picture is becoming clear in my mind. Religion will somehow have to meet the social needs of its believers and satisfy their need for community action and involvement. Future religion will be much more about the HERE and much less about the hereafter. New or reformed religions will have a much reduced need for clergy and hierarchy. The role they fill is likely to be more representative of the faithful, rather than of the head guru.

Future religions will likely respect and incorporate today's great religions and exist with them in harmony. New religion needs to ditch the dogmatic. It's becoming clear that no longer is man's best friend a dogma.

Religion seems destined to propagate, grow, and endure, using the internet as well as the cable TV model of hundreds of specialty channels. There almost certainly will be more than the tens of thousands of religious denominations, cults, and sects that exist already. This multitude of religions will be financed more along the lines of public TV subscription drives than of pass-the-basket collections of yesterday. The current televangelist fund drives are one possible model. Not-for-profit foundations seem likely to play a larger and larger quasi-religious role.

I predict we will finally realize that no one has the corner on Truth. New religion won't claim the right of un-doubt-ability. In science and life, our truths are valid only until replaced with better information. It is unlikely to be any different for religion or our beliefs about a Divine Being. Reasonable probability works in virtually all areas of our lives. It will have to do in religion.

Know-it-alls are insufferable in academic and social situations. Why should they be tolerated in religion? Ultimately, dogmatism will be seen to be passé. (Our karma will run over our dogma?)

Somehow we need to find a balance of openness, believability, even acceptance of others' religious points of view. We have to find a balance between our seemingly self-indulgent, personal/situational ethics and the classic principles found in existing world religions. As Diana Eck puts it,

The challenge we all face is to build a world-wide culture of pluralism in which our differences become the source of our vibrancy and strength.… If we can succeed, this legacy… will be the greatest form of lasting leadership we can offer the world.

What about the old, comfortable ritual and ceremony? In ancient and modern organized religions, they clearly satisfy a need. They tell a story. They suggest credibility and authority. They maintain tradition. They satisfy the need for beauty and grandeur. They inspire. They stimulate imagination. They fill needs for both complexity and simplicity. They provide both mystery and resolution. Some say the Catholic Church has endured not only for the message, but also for the presentation that filled many human needs.

George Fox, founder of the Quakers, says of the cathedrals, "The Lord showed me, so that I did see clearly, that he did not dwell in these temples which men had commanded and set up, but in people's hearts… his people were his temple, and he dwelt in them."

Temples may not be inherently sacred, but the community they house seems to be an essential element to any religion—at least a *sense* of community. Certainly, the major religions surviving today include regular gatherings of like-minded folks. Community also facilitates more effective political or social group action.

Pluralism also seems essential. Multiple-choice in religion (like history tests) seems to work best. A single, dogmatic concept of God clearly invites conflicts.

So, is the New Age religion of every man and woman for him- or herself the way to go? Since the 1960s, it seems as though the watch words have been "if it feels good, do it" or "believe it." In the case of the current evangelists, it is "if you build it (the crystal cathedral or the TV network), they will come." These dated, and soon-to-be-dated, abusive fixes of traditional organized religions are beginning to leave people cold because they realize they're being led to a quasi-reformed religion that ultimately proves unsatisfying. Religions that satisfy only a selfish, personal need are not enough.

Abraham Maslow said it well in the 1960s:

> The search for the exotic, the strange, the unusual, the uncommon has often taken the form of pilgrimages, of turning away from the world, the "Journey to the East," to another country or to a different Religion. The great lesson from the true mystics …[is] that the sacred is *in* the ordinary, that it is to be found in one's daily life, in one's neighbors, friends, and family…. To be looking elsewhere for miracles is… a sure sign of ignorance that *everything* is miraculous.

A contemporary twist in the search for daily, run-of-the-mill miracles is described in *A Course in Miracles* (ACIM), which assumes that human perfection is the only possibility because we are created by God. This approach to religion is largely internal and personal, looking inside our "Self" and overcoming our own egos. Based largely on the Christian Bible model, it is practical and logical, rather than a dogmatic interpretation. Compassion and forgiveness toward others as well as conquering our ego are the action steps recommended. Self-study, rather than reliance on an institutional church, is the suggested approach.

An increasingly popular alternative to the approach of organized religion is the action-oriented, not-for-profit organization. This model looks much like an entrepreneurial business. Many such groups have adopted the highest moral values of world religions and, notably, act on these values. They've combine good business practices with compassion and practical, religious-type values. In addition, many specifically focus on helping people help themselves. Often they make good examples for the reform of organized religion.

One example of nonprofit social activism is the Grameen Bank. In 2006, Dr. Muhammad Yunus from Bangladesh was awarded the Nobel Peace Prize for being the granddaddy of the microcredit marketplace and starting a trend toward full banking services for the poor.

FINCA (www.villagebanking.org) is another example that takes a high-leverage, sustainable approach to philanthropy by making small loans to poor entrepreneurial women in developing countries. No dogma, just dollars (which have to be paid back) describes FINCA's plan to encourage self-help. I visited three village banks in Guatemala City barrios and was impressed with the business acumen of the forty or so women members. With short-term loans of $50 to $250, these women bought supplies and inventory: corn flour to make tortillas to sell door-to-door; shoes, clothes, or restaurant supplies to resell in little shops. The founder's motto is "Give poor communities the opportunity, and then get out of the way!" The emphasis is on teaching women to fish, and I believe the founding prophets would approve.

Heifer International (www.heifer.org) does similar work in the form of providing livestock breeding pairs to poor villagers around the world. The deal is, some of the animals' offspring are in turn contributed to fellow villagers ("passing on the gift") in a self-sustaining program model. The object is to end world hunger in an environmentally friendly way. Heifer's website says the group "has worked from the very beginning with faith communities following all spiritual paths."

Rotary International is one of the oldest and most ambitious not-for-profit organizations. The large sums of contributed cash are virtually always supplemented by face-to-face volunteer work by some of the 1.2 million worldwide members from 32,000 clubs in 200 countries. One nearly accomplished goal is the elimination of polio worldwide. By 2003, Rotary had raised $118 million to eradicate polio. Clubs typically support their own communities in education and health-improvement projects. Its motto is "Service above Self" (no dogma declared).

Not-for-profits or non-government organizations (NGOs) collectively don't come close to matching U.S. and Western nations' foreign aid (according to one source, $2.3 trillion over the last five decades). The Catholic Church and other organized religions also make major charitable investments. However, the not-for-profit money is often especially well spent, with good leverage for sustainable self-help programs.

Many of these not-for-profit cases are great examples of "actions speaking louder than dogma." Acting on the religious principles of compassion and help for the poor, they have tapped into an individual and political responsibility to effectively offer help. Institutional religions might take note: downsize the dogma; cut the creed; reduce the ritual; and accelerate the action of the here-and-now part of their missions.

Historically, religions haven't needed to reform because they have held a virtual monopoly in their marketplaces. Well, all of that has changed and it is time to focus on the realities of the twenty-first century needs of religious communities and the needs of the whole world community. Many folks seem to want more effective action from religion and are willing to ditch the dogma to get it.

# SERMON ON THE MOLEHILL

*Teach me but don't preach me.*

Each of our lives is about choices. We're dealt a nation, a family, a neighborhood, a school, and usually a religion. Our playing cards are not equal. Mostly, in the beginning, we just hold our cards. We don't know we have choices. Gradually—some sooner, some later—we make incidental choices about family and friends, about our personality. During and after high school and maybe college, we begin making life choices about jobs and mates and where to live. A few of us go on to make choices about country and religion and spiritual life. With respect to these last three, most of us decide not to decide.

I remained a dogma-bound-and-gagged Catholic through high school, college, and early military service. Then I saw some non-Catholic points of view. At age thirty, I unconverted and have spent the years since as a fallen away. I decided then what to leave, but not where to go next.

I've never seriously doubted God because I could never accept our universe as an accident. But I doubt my—or anyone's, for that matter— ability to ever understand God. I very seriously doubt organized religions' claim to understand and explain the Almighty.

A monopoly on truth seems forever unlikely. No church, no government, no parent, no lawyer or court, not even Hollywood, will ever be all knowing. We can only hope to gather bits of information and decide for ourselves.

Google "God" on the Internet and you'll get nearly six hundred million entries in one-tenth of a second. That is the number I got in January 2008. (But I only got two hundred and seventy million in one-eighteenth of a second in July 2013). Surely we have enough information today. We've gone from too little data to too much. Sorting and verifying can be a challenge, but we're becoming adept at evaluating daily torrents of data. When it comes to religion, what good does it get us?

For help evaluating, we can use and appreciate the wisdom of the living saints who focus on the spiritual. You know them and respect them: Mother Theresa types; the kind friend who is always willing to help; maybe your own mother, father, or family member. And we can turn to those devoting their lives to raising the spiritual consciousness of our world or even their own neighborhoods. They are all around us.

But beware of spiritual perpetual-motion machines. Spirituality without a commitment to social and political action in the here and now is all show and no go: "All of this is no more than sounding brass and tinkling cymbals unless you have love [act lovingly]." (I Corinthians 13:1) The Qur'an, too, stresses our obligation to help orphans, widows without support, and those less fortunate.

Beware, as well, of church-appointed saints focused only inward toward their personal vision of God. They often don't seem to notice the world around them. They may be holy, but by modern definition they can be considered self-centered egotists, praised and be-sainted by ecclesiasts focused on the perpetuation of their own exclusionary religious myth. Okay, maybe that's a little harsh. A more optimistic view is that we are all saints in training.

Seek out the saints around you. Chopra says it well in *How to Know God*: "Reality changes at different stages of growth. At some level everyone knows the highest truth. Everyone is doing the best they can from their own level of consciousness." And he also says, "The actual goal of spiritual life [is] to free humans and allow them to live in innocence and love."

Choose spiritual activists as friends. Our religious founding fathers were all *action* heroes. They chose to challenge and change the unjust societies into which they were born. We are not talking about a bunch of introverts—these religious entrepreneurs attended to real-life, daily, social injustice.

Choose those important values classic religions bring to the twenty-first century. Abraham Maslow calls them "final values" and "principles of choice which help us to answer the age-old 'spiritual'… questions." And he elaborates on the nature of these questions:

> What is the good life: What is the good man? The good woman? What is the good society and what is my relation to it? What is best for my children? What is justice? Truth? Virtue? What is my relation to nature, to death, to aging, to pain, to illness? How can I

live a zestful, enjoyable, meaningful life? What is my responsibility to my brothers?

Who are my brothers? What shall I be loyal to? What must I be ready to die for?

...It used to be that all these questions were answered by organized religions in their various ways. Slowly these answers have come more and more to be based on natural, empirical fact and less and less on custom, tradition, "revelations," sacred texts, interpretations by a priestly class.

Choose new information from sources you trust. To be more trustworthy, reformed religions must be more accountable. They must measure themselves and be judged by their faithful: do they achieve social justice and relieve suffering and poverty? Are they transparent and open in the conduct of their clergy, in the state of their finances, and in the practice of their spirituality? Government, business, and life all trend toward openness, albeit sometimes kicking and screaming. For their own survival, religions—especially Big Business, Big Politic religions—must join the more transparent world.

For our own long-term best interests, we need compassion in our capitalistic and competitive culture; justice not only for the lawyer-enabled well-to-do, but for all developing and developed nations lacking personal freedoms. Truth, loyalty, tolerance, respect, and acceptance of contrary beliefs need to be more than just social niceties. Ethical and personal obligations are essential to millennium religion. We must act like Jesus, Buddha, Muhammad, Moses, and the models of our civilization. The spiritual and religious evolution envisioned by all great religious prophets and founders must be nourished and expanded. We need to continue inside or outside the religions that grew from the prophets' teachings. We need to put a viable HERE in the classic religions' ideal hereafter. We need to lead, and hope organized world religion follows.

We need to believe in our own God. We need to act in our own Spinozan "enlightened self-interest." Our spiritual and physical well-being is tied to our fellow passengers on this traveling planet. We need to love our earth neighbors as we love ourselves, and not wait for nor count on divine intervention.

Albert Einstein once said, "I believe in Spinoza's God who reveals

Himself in the orderly harmony of what exists, not in a God who concerns Himself with fates and actions of human beings."

We each can borrow a bit of spirituality from the great classic world religions or from one of the thousands of spiritual start-ups. We can now decide on our personal brand of spirituality. We can individually contribute to the world spiritual pool.

Belief in a higher order, a supreme good, a benevolent God, the fundamental value of people and nature are important. But belief alone is not enough. In religion, like in business, politics, and life (including raising kids), it is "show me, don't just tell me." We need to act on our beliefs.

We've all looked for the magic fix—from parents, teachers, friends, or mate. But as we mature, we realize our own daily choices make the difference.

No matter what we call God, Allah, or whatever, most of the world agrees on the basics. Virtually all religions believe in an absolute spiritual force. If we can accept the single, simple principle of progressive revelation (or progressive creation), we've got a chance at religious peace in our times. Organized religions build on or disagree with earlier knowledge, revelation, practices, and beliefs. If we accept knowledge in religion as evolving in the manner of science, art, literature, and all other forms of human knowledge, we can move from doctrinaire toward progressive enlightenment. We can enlighten our self-interests. We can progressively create.

Creation didn't just happen once, as in the biblical sense. Creation is on-going. It continues today and every day.

We can minimize, forgive, or make light of our foibles, insignificant difference, and endearing eccentricities. And we can be serious, intense, and joyful about shared love and respect for each other. We can relish and foster our spiritual ties and rich religious diversity.

Easy to say, but what do these platitudes mean in practical terms? What's the bottom line for us 7 billion squabbling earthlings? Well, if we didn't have to fight about religion, maybe we wouldn't need to fight at all. "Live and let live" alone could save us about a trillion dollars per year, according to the 2004 *World-wide Military Spending Estimate* (globalsecurity.org).

Does this mean to cut police and military, and suffer attack by rampaging hordes? No, we need protection until we can all get on the same enlightened page. Bad actors will always need to be reined in. But selling their adventures at playing God will become increasingly difficult as we each come to trust our own spiritual judgment and belief.

Imagine a world in which we saved half of all current military budgets. That would leave five hundred billion dollars annually for Christian, Muslim, Jewish, non-profit, and other control-tab effective philanthropy. Half the world lives on less than two dollars a day. Five hundred billion dollars divided by 2.8 billion poor people is ninety times what they currently live on. Think of the possibilities: immediate food and health care, plus education and economic infrastructure. Might that be a better bargain for our investment?

This means rejecting pandering politicians who play on our fears and try to convince us that they and government are our only hope, and rejecting religious leaders who do the same. Our important personal responsibility is to know there is no such thing as zero physical or spiritual risk and to be brave and confident in our free future. We must demand respect for our beliefs and our civic-friendly personal choices.


How does that translate into modern life and daily issues? We make choices based on the religion or non-religion that works for us. If we are committed to a compassionate and just society, how do we act day-to-day?

Suppose we get up in the morning and walk down to a coffee shop for a cup of brew (coffee, silly). Are the workers there getting a decent, livable wage? If not, perhaps they are getting an opportunity to learn some skills on or off the job in addition to their wage. Is that refreshing cup of coffee provided at the expense of a poor grower who is being taken advantage of—one who is being penalized by agricultural, protectionist subsidies by our own government (read the "2013 Farm Bill")?

Not to sound like a pinko-commie utopian, but do we ignore the ethics of daily choices because we are numb, or maybe just because we haven't connected the dots?

Many of us are involved as members of various popular movements. We work to save the planet, protect animals, and especially to foster peace among seemingly unconscious and at-war humans. But, in the manner of *A Course in Miracles*, Eckhart Tolle warns we cannot fight unconsciousness without becoming less conscious ourselves and strengthening the warring polar opposites. Rather, in *The Power of Now*, he recommends,

> Raise awareness by disseminating information, or at the most, practice passive resistance. But make sure that you carry no resistance within, no hatred, no negativity. "Love your enemies," said Jesus, which, of course, means "have no enemies."
>
> …Once you get involved in working on the level of effect, it is all too easy to lose yourself in it. Stay alert and very, very present. The causal level needs to remain your primary focus, the teaching of enlightenment your main purpose, and peace your most precious gift to the world.

As distasteful as it may seem to those who have been turned off by the abuses, political involvement is required. We tend to ignore local, state, and national politics, except briefly and sometimes trivially near election time. But big bucks are spent even by your county government; the current budget where I live, in San Mateo County, California (720,000 population), is more than $1.7 billion per year. Some money spent by local, state, and federal governments is earmarked wisely and some is not. Like big religion, big government spends a lot on just maintaining the organization and often has only limited accountability. But if we want to apply the control tab factor to leveraging our civic (and perhaps religious) values, there is no more important place to start than politics.

For example, how does our spirituality or choice of religion translate into action on foreign wars, or to the war on drugs, or to the issue of stem cell research, or on illegal immigration, or protecting our natural environment? Among participants of organized religions or people with civic values derived from world religions, opinion diverges widely on just these issues.

Is the cost of war in dollars and lives worth the results? Was the enormous cost of World War II worth stopping Hitler and ending the Holocaust? Would it have been moral not to get involved? Was the cost of the Iraq war morally acceptable to free Iraqis from the terror of Saddam Hussein? How about to protect our oil supply? Does organized religion today provide clear guidance on the key moral issues we face now? Depending on which religion and which branch (liberal or conservative), a believer is likely to get very different answers, or no answer at all, to these moral dilemmas. We will have to personally decide in every case.

If we find a spirituality or new and evolving religion that works and that we can embrace, will we personally change? Most of us are not movers and shakers, but every day we each make hundreds of choices that can make us more compassionate and just, or less. My sister-in-law Maries relays a Native American story. One evening an old Cherokee told his grandson about a battle that goes on inside people. He said,

> "My son, the battle is between two 'wolves' inside us all. One is Evil. It is anger, envy, jealousy, sorrow, regret, greed, arrogance, self-pity, guilt, resentment, inferiority, lies, false pride, superiority, and ego. The other is Good. It is joy, peace, love, hope, serenity, humility, kindness, benevolence, empathy, generosity, truth, compassion and faith."
>
> The grandson thought about it for a minute and then asked his grandfather, "Which wolf wins?"
>
> The old Cherokee simply replied, "The one you feed."

We are not likely to author a new Emancipation Proclamation or Papal Encyclical or Brown vs. the Board of Education court precedent. But many small-scale, personal decisions led to each of those dramatic social changes. Those were individual decisions about acting to change the same kinds of injustice and cruelty we watch nightly on TV.

We've recently seen amazing advances in science and medicine, in teaching methods, in government improvements and industry reform. But how much have we advanced human happiness and peace? How much more advanced and pervasive is brotherhood and sisterhood today than it was twenty-five or fifty or a hundred years ago? How much progress have we made in eliminating poverty and extending human freedoms?

Our lack of progress may be because we have been paying too much attention to the trivia and minutiae and the form and ritual of an idealized religious life. And our progress may be minimal because we've followed world religions' emphasis on the hereafter rather than on the original HERE of the founders. Could we be missing the macro picture? The great prophets all lived their lives with present-moment consciousness and preached about an ideal life that was grounded in a fully present world. Their talk about the hereafter was relatively incidental to the manner in which they wanted us to treat our fellow flesh-and-blood humans every day. What would happen if we acted more in line with the great, simple, essential, daily-action life principles of the world religions— instead of with their dogma, doctrine, and ritual?

Will those world religions re-form again and return to the roots of their founding geniuses? If we are a member of a major religion, what is our obligation to act to reform it, to make it more compassionate and accountable?

We have always identified with God in an image, be it Moses, Jesus, Muhammad, or others. Not surprising, because how else could we mere humans really imagine God? By definition, God is beyond our powers of imagination and reasoning. Maybe the question is: can we best imagine God as an ideal us? Is God within us just waiting to be let out? If we can begin to imagine a perfect self, do we start to imagine God? Would that help us see God HERE, where it matters, instead of just in some distant hereafter?


As grown-ups, we realize sports and film and political heroes all have feet of clay. But we seem to honor them as the best we have. We have had real human heroes whom we see as approaching god-like or ideal human beings: the prophets, Lincoln, Gandhi, and others. And we've created many imaginary heroes, such as Superman and Wonder Woman.

Billions practice hero worship for the great prophets of all time. Now we can begin to see God in our hearts and in the hearts of humankind. Is that all the great prophets were really asking—for us to see God in ourselves and in our fellow humans? All the great prophets encouraged us to *act* the good life. They all said *do* good for ourselves and others, especially for those others less able.

In the words of a local meditation group's website, "The development of compassionate action does not stop with non-harming. An active compassion which wishes to help others can take many forms in the world, such as social work, community development, or political or environmental activism."

God or Allah by any other name is still God. How shall we worship Him or Her: At all? In a church, mosque, or synagogue? In our own private way? In a way not yet discovered? Shall we see and believe in the God within, the God in our hearts? If we see the God within and the God within others, can we then act our age, act our potential?

There is no better opportunity than right now to find common ground about religion and God. We've gone on separate tracks for generations, but all the while it has been really toward the same destination: a peaceful, productively virtuous life on earth, and for many, the prospect of a life hereafter. Let's build on and appreciate the great good and enormous progress of world religions *and* the independent quest for spirituality, in God's name.

Like expanding our appreciation of art and music, we can grow our knowledge, understanding, acceptance, and even love of the *principles* of all the world's great religions. I believe the benefits can be ginormous.

For me, the journey has only just started and already I see world religion and spirituality in a different—a brighter— light. I began with dangerous misconceptions, especially about Islam. Due to my reading, watching, and listening, those misconceptions have been dispelled. I've come to believe we are all more alike than apart in our basic beliefs. Surely, as rich and poor, as Christian, Muslim, Hindu, Jew, or Buddhist, we are not dealt the same playing cards, physically, economically, and spiritually speaking. But regardless of our religion or non-religion, a strong argument can be made that God exists within each of us and that we are simply on different spiritual paths (or non-paths) to the same destination. And it is not a mountain top or high in the sky. It can be found in the human heart.

It's clear there is no one immutable truth about God, at least not one we mere humans can discern. Let's humbly admit our ignorance and acknowledge our long-term reliance on others' interpretations and opinions about God. It's time to set all that aside. With the benefit of mounds of information about all religions and spiritual roads now more accessible than ever, we can finally make free and informed choices from among the many interpretations of the messages of the great prophets. We can decide and act on our own.

Perhaps, just perhaps, we can expand our knowledge and consciousness in the direction of becoming a unified world family. Again, for me, this began with the recognition that I actually have choices. I can personally decide what spirituality means for me. I can act on and live out my beliefs as I see fit. Once I accepted this power of choice, a whole universe opened and I saw the charm and beauty of the myriad religious and spiritual points of view.

Conversion is not required—neither to anything nor from anything. I believe it's more about all the little choices we make every day. It's about awareness of the people and things around us. It's about recognizing God (or Good, for you devout atheists) in our spouse, our family, friends, and neighbors. It seems we can only hope to find Love by choosing to *act* on our conscious and loving spiritual choices.

Each of the great prophets had a vision, a profound experience of the divine. Each shared that vision with the people of the time, in the language of that era. The audience for these messages was generally illiterate and undoubtedly appreciated and stood in awe of these human interpretations of God.

Today we have the benefit of these ancient and profound descriptions of the divine, augmented by the interpretations of holy men and women as well as many kooks and zealots. We've had folks along the way who not only claimed to speak for God, but who claimed they were the one-and-only God. Given their abundant other not-so-endearing human characteristics, we've usually been able to recognize the charlatans. During the same period of time, we've added to our knowledge of the sciences and bolstered the store of human learning.

This has placed us in a unique historical position. If we truly begin to exercise our freedom of spiritual choice, we will see God in many, many different ways. This is a good thing. Sure, the Pope and his counterpart religious leadership may have superior intellectual knowledge (school learnin') about theology. But is their vision of the divine really clearer than that of all the rest of us? Organized religion's approach has too often been like the sophists' endless debate about how many angels can dance on the head of a pin. Centuries of intellectual energy expended on defending dogma has added little to our personal, useful vision of the God of here and now.

Well, you ask, what about all the pain and evil in this world, which is the focus of so much organized religion?

I say, we have a choice. We can believe in fallen angels turned devils, or we can believe all humans are doing the best they can at their stage of consciousness, that they have yet to uncover the vision of God in themselves and in others. Occam and I prefer the latter explanation. It's much simpler. And it relieves so much needless suffering. It takes away the dogmatic directive to see evil where there may really be none.

We may not believe we can control our ultimate destiny, but it is clear we get to make many choices each day. And each conscious choice shapes and reshapes our lives, bringing us (hopefully) closer to God or human perfection.

I'm not saying we're so smart we can now know God. My own feeling is that I can no more understand the divine than an amoeba can understand an antelope. But I do believe we all can see the signs of God in ourselves and each other. We can see that God-ness and goodness are built into our DNA. And most important, regardless of what we think we know, we can't lose if we always *act* as if we know God is within us, within all other human beings, and within all of nature.

# REFERENCES

**Introduction**
Deck, Rev. E. M. 1930. *Baltimore catechism, No. 1*. Buffalo, NY: Rauch & Stoeckl.

## SECTION 1

**Religion Gets Organized**
James, William. 1987. *Writings—1902-1910: The varieties of religious experience*. New York: Library of America. 444.

## SECTION 2

**My Religion Is Better than Yours**
Haleem, M. A. S. Abdel. 2004. *The Qur'an*. New York: Oxford University Press.
Torrey, R. A. ed. 1994. *The fundamentals: A testimony to the truth*. Grand Rapids, MI: Baker Book House.
Wallis, Jim. 2005. *God's politics: Why the right gets it wrong and the left doesn't get it*. San Francisco: HarperOne.

**Religious Zealots, Fanatics, and Terrorists**
Hoffer, Eric. 1972. Thoughts of Eric Hoffer, including: Absolute faith corrupts absolutely. *The New York Times Magazine*. April 25.
Stern, Jessica. 2004. *Terror in the name of God: Why religious militants kill*. New York: HarperCollins. xix.
CBS News. 2003. *Terror in the name of God: Author examines the connection between religion and terrorism*. August 20. http://www.cbsnews.com/stories/2003/08/19/earlyshow/leisure/books/main569179.shtml (accessed January 1, 2008).
*9/11 Commission report*. 2004. Washington DC: U.S. Government Printing

Office. http://www.gpoaccess.gov/911/index.html (accessed January 1, 2008).

Hassan, Nasra. 2001. An arsenal of believers: Talking to the human bombs. *The New Yorker.* November 19. http://www.newyorker.com/fact/content/articles/011119fa_FA CT1 (accessed January 1, 2008).

Pape, Robert. 2005. The logic of suicide terrorism: It's the occupation, not the fundamentalism. *The American Conservative.* July 18. http://www.amconmag.com/2005_07_18/article.html (accessed January 1, 2008).

Pipes, Daniel. 2003. [Finding moderate Muslims:] Do you believe in modernity? *Jerusalem Post.* November 26. http://www.danielpipes.org/article/1322 (accessed January 1, 2008).

Steyn, Mark. 2005. Islam's major export: Don't worry, they have baseball bats. *National Review.* November 21. 64. http://article.nationalreview.com/?q=NTVjYzhlZTE2YzY4ZmM2YTRhYTY2MmRiMWNmM2Y0MGM= (accessed January 1, 2008).

Alexiev, Alex. 2005. What it takes: If we are to win the War on Terror, we must do far more. *National Review.* November 7.

Twain, Mark. 2004. *Letters from the Earth: Uncensored writings.* Ed. Bernard DeVoto. New York and Evanston, IL: Harper & Row. 237.

Friedman, Thomas. L. 2005. Giving the hatemongers no place to hide. *The New York Times.* July 22. http://www.nytimes.com/2005/07/22/opinion/22friedman.html (accessed January 1, 2008).

## SECTION 3

### Judaism

Crim, Keith, Roger A. Bullard, and Larry D. Shinn, eds. 1981. *The perennial dictionary of world religions.* New York: HarperCollins.

Telushkin, Rabbi Joseph. 2001. *Jewish literacy.* New York: HarperCollins.

### Hinduism

Crim, Keith, Roger A. Bullard, and Larry D. Shinn, eds. 1981. *The perennial dictionary of world religions.* New York: HarperCollins.

Bly, Robert, trans. 2004. *Kabir: Ecstatic poems.* Boston: Beacon Press. 52.

Allen, John, L. 2005. He was a magnificent pope who presided over a controversial pontificate. *National Catholic Reporter.* April 15 http:// www.nationalcatholicreporter.org/update/conclave/jp_obi t_main. htm (accessed January 1, 2008).

Ontario Consultants on Religious Tolerance. n.d. *Hinduism: Additional information & links.* Religioustolerance.org, http://www. religioustolerance.org/hinduism3.htm (accessed January 1, 2008).

## Traditional Chinese Religions

Crim, Keith, Roger A. Bullard, and Larry D. Shinn, eds. 1981. *The perennial dictionary of world religions.* New York: HarperCollins.

Legge, James. 2004. *Life and teachings of Confucius.* Whitefish, MT: Kessinger. 137.

## Buddhism

Crim, Keith, Roger A. Bullard, and Larry D. Shinn, eds. 1981. *The perennial dictionary of world religions.* New York: HarperCollins.

Hanh, Thich Nhat. 1995. *Living Buddha, Living Christ.* New York, Penguin Putnam. 54.

## Christianity

Barrett, David B., George T. Kurian, and Todd M. Johnson, eds. 2001. *World Christian encyclopedia: A comparative survey of churches and religions in the modern world.* New York: Oxford University Press.

Senior , Donald, and John J. Collins, eds. 1990. *The Catholic study Bible: New American Bible.* New York: Oxford University Press.

## Islam

Abou El Fadl, Khaled M. 2005. *The great theft.* New York: HarperCollins. 18-20.

*Major branches of religions ranked by number of adherents.* n.d. http://www. adherents.com/adh_branches.html#Islam (accessed January 1, 2008).

Haleem, M. A. S. Abdel. 2004. *The Qur'an.* New York: Oxford University Press.

Crim, Keith, Roger A. Bullard, and Larry D. Shinn, eds. 1981. *The perennial dictionary of world religions.* New York: HarperCollins.

## Baha'i

Bahá'u'lláh. 1992. *The kitáb-i-aqdas: The most holy book.* Bahá'í World Centre. http://reference.bahai.org/en/t/b/KA/ (accessed January 1, 2008). 75.

*What is the* Bahá'í *faith?* 2007. Bahá'í International Community http://www.bahai.org/faq/facts/bahai_faith (accessed January 1, 2008).

## None of the Above

Taylor, Humphrey. 2003. While most Americans believe in God, only 36% attend a religious service once a month or more often. *The Harris Poll, No. 59.* October 15. http://www.harrisinteractive.com/harris_poll/index.asp?PID=40 8 (accessed January 1, 2008).

Fox, Richard Wightman. 2006. *Lincoln's religious quest: Why his faith won't suit either side in the culture wars.* http://www.slate.com/id/2134450/ (accessed January 1, 2008).

Wilson, Edwin H. 1995. *Genesis of a humanist manifesto.* Amherst, NY: Humanist Press.

Smith, Sam. 2005. Seventh Day Adventists arise: You have nothing to lose but your stereotype. *Progressive Review.* April 11. http://www.prorev.com/agnostic.htm (accessed January 1, 2008).

Peterson, Merrill, ed. 1997. *Thomas Jefferson: Writings.* New York: Library of America. 509–10.

Orlov, Tatiana. 2005. *79% say good people of other faiths can go to heaven, according to new Newsweek/beliefnet poll.* August 22. http://www.beliefnet.com/releases/Newsweek- beliefnetpollfinal.pdf (accessed January 1, 2008).

Forman, Samuel E., ed. 1900. *The life and writing of Thomas Jefferson.* Indianapolis, IN: Bowen-Merrill.

Hadaway C. Kirk, and P. L. Marler. 1998. Did you really go to church this week? Behind the poll data. *The Christian Century.* May 6. 472–475 http://www.religion-online.org/showarticle.asp?title=237 (accessed January 1, 2008).

Robinson, B. A. *How The concepts of God have developed over the ages.* Ontario Consultants on Religious Tolerance. http://www.religioustolerance.org/god_devel.htm (accessed January 1, 2008).

Newport, Frank. 2006. Estimating Americans' worship behavior.

*Gallup.com.* January 3. http://www.gallup.com/poll/20701/Estimating-Americans- Worship-Behavior.aspx (accessed January 1, 2008).

Belief-O-Matic: A personality quiz about your religious and spiritual beliefs.

*Beliefnet.com.* http://www.beliefnet.com/story/76/story_7665_1.html (accessed January 1, 2008).

Olsen, Burke. 2002. Americans struggle with religion's role at home and abroad. *The Pew Forum on Religion and Public Life.* March 20. http://pewforum.org/press/index.php?ReleaseID=13 (accessed January 1, 2008).

Barrett, David B., George T. Kurian, and Todd M. Johnson, eds. 2001. *World Christian encyclopedia: A comparative survey of churches and religions in the modern world.* New York: Oxford University Press.

Spong, John Shelby. 1999. *Why Christianity must change or die: A bishop speaks to believers in exile.* San Francisco: Harper.

Armstrong, Karen. 2001. *Muhammad: A biography of the prophet.* San Francisco: Harper.

Aslan, Reza. 2005. *No god but God: The origins, evolution, and future of Islam.* New York: Random House.

Dawkins, Richard. 2006. *The God delusion,* New York: Houghton Mifflin. Hitchens, Christopher. 2007. *God is not great: How religion poisons everything.* New York: Hachette Book Group.

Harris, Sam. 2006. *Letter to a Christian nation.* New York: Knopf.

## SECTION 4

### Change from Within

James, William. 1987. *Writings—1902-1910: The varieties of religious experience.* New York: Library of America. 305-6.

Chopra, Deepak. 2005. *Peace is the way.* New York: Three Rivers Press. 156.

### Christian Reform

Blueprint for Vatican III: Catholics worldwide map church future. 2002. *National Catholic Reporter.* May 3. http://www.findarticles.com/p/articles/mi_m1141/is_26_38/ai_ 86047262 (accessed January 1, 2008).

Barna, George. 2005. *Revolution: Finding vibrant faith beyond the walls of sanctuary.* Carol Stream, IL: Tyndale House. 9-16, 37-9, 104.

Spong, John Shelby. 1999. *Why Christianity must change or die.* San Francisco: Harper, 226-27.

Spong, John Shelby. 1992. *Rescuing the Bible from fundamentalism.* San

Francisco: Harper.

Eckhart, Tolle. 1999. *The power of now: A guide to spiritual enlightenment.* Novato, CA: New World Library. 87.

Sheehan, Thomas. 1986. *First coming: How the kingdom of God became Christianity.* New York: Random House. 61.

## Muslim Reform

Shirin, Ebadi. 2003. *In the name of the God of creation and wisdom.* Nobel lecture, Oslo. December 10. http://nobelprize.org/nobel_prizes/ peace/laureates/2003/ebadi- lecture-e.html (accessed January 1, 2008).

Heim, S. Mark. 2004. A different kind of Islamic state. *The Christian Century.*, October 5. 30-3. http://www.religion-

online.org/showarticle.asp?title=3136 (accessed January 1, 2008). Charny, Israel W. 2006. *Fighting suicide bombing: A worldwide campaign for life.*

Westport, CT: Praeger. 43.

Suicide bomber cleric Yusuf Qaradawi issues fatwa warning "Anyone who kills a dhimmi will not smell the fragrance of paradise!" 2005. *Militant Islam Monitor.* July 28. http://www.militantislammonitor.org/ article/id/873 (accessed January 1, 2008).

Chang, Momo. 2005. *SF Bay Area Muslims pledge to fight hate in mosques.*

Islamic Society of North America. July 20. http://isna.net/index. php?backPID=5&id=35&tt_news=253 (accessed January 1, 2008).

Rushdie, Salman. 2000. *The satanic verses: A novel.* New York: Picador. Rushdie: Islam needs reformation. 2005. *Middle East Online.* August 11.

http://middle-east-online.com/english/Default.pl?id=14259 (accessed January 1, 2008).

Zoll, Rachael. 2005. Muslim scholars declare terrorism a violation of Islam. *The Boston Globe.* July 29. http://www.boston.com/news/nation/ articles/2005/07/29/mus lim_scholars_declare_terrorism_a_ violation_of_islam/ (accessed January 1, 2008).

Nunn, Sam. 2005. Speech at the Commonwealth Club, San Francisco. November 15.

Kepel, Gilles. 2004. *The war for Muslim minds: Islam and the West.* Cambridge, MA: Belknap Press.

## One or Many

Aslan, Reza. 2005. *No god but God: The origins, evolution, and future of Islam.* New York: Random House. 263.

Borg, Marcus J. 2003. *The heart of Christianity.* New York: HarperCollins. 120-1.

Heim, S. Mark. 2004. A different kind of Islamic state. *The Christian Century.*, October 5. 30-3. http://www.religion-online.org/showarticle.asp?title=3136 (accessed January 1, 2008).

Eck, Diana L. 2002. *A new religious America: Managing religious diversity in a democracy: Challenges and prospects for the 21st century.* Keynote address at Kuala Lumpur, Malaysia, August 20-1. http://www.usembassymalaysia.org.my/eck.html (accessed January 1, 2008).

Eck, Diana L. 2002. A new religious America: How a "Christian country" has become the world's most religiously diverse nation. San Francisco: HarperOne.

Trent, William Peterfield, John Erskine, Stuart P. Sherman, and Carl Van Doren, eds. 1921. *The Cambridge history of American literature.* New York: G. P. Putnam. 373.

Wallis, Jim. *God's politics: Why the right gets it wrong and the left doesn't get it.* San Francisco: HarperOne. xxvi, 241.

Potts, Michel W. 2002. Arun Gandhi shares the Mahatma's message. *India-West.* San Leandro, CA. (1 February) 27(13): A34.

## Actions Speak Louder Than Dogma

Toms, Justine Willis. 2003. Trim [Control] tab factor: Tiny changes that make the world a better place. *Awakened Woman: The Journal of Women's Spirituality.* October 29. http://www.awakenedwoman.com/toms_trim_tab.htm (accessed January 1, 2008).

Maslow, Abraham. 1970. *Religions, values, and peak-experiences.* New York: Penguin. 4, 33, 43.

Armstrong, Karen. 1993. *A history of God.* New York: Random House. 17, 33, 234-39, 397-8.

Tallentyre, S.G., trans. 1919. *Voltaire in his letters.* New York: Putnam. http://en.wikiquote.org/wiki/Voltaire (accessed January 1, 2008).

Chopra, Deepak. 2000. *How to know God, The soul's journey into the mystery of mysteries.* New York: Random House. 175.

Eck, Diana L. 2002. *A new religious America: Managing religious diversity in a democracy: Challenges and prospects for the 21st century.* Keynote address at Kuala Lumpur, Malaysia, August 20-1. http://www. usembassymalaysia.org.my/eck.html (accessed January 1, 2008).

Federer, William Joseph. 1994. *America's God and country: Encyclopedia of quotations.* St Louis: MO. Amerisearch. 238.

Maslow, Abraham. 1993. *The farther reaches of human nature.* New York: Penguin. 345.

Schucman, Helen, and William Thetford, eds. 1992. *A course in miracles.* Mill Valley, CA: Foundation for Inner Peace. viii-ix.

## Sermon on the Molehill

Chopra, Deepak. 2000. *How to know God, The soul's journey into the mystery of mysteries.* New York: Random House. 83, 191.

Maslow, Abraham. 1970. *Religions, values, and peak-experiences.* New York: Penguin. 52.

Schilpp, Paul Arthur, ed. 1970. *Albert Einstein: Philosopher-scientist.* 3rd ed. La Salle, IL: The Open Court Publishing. 659-60.

Eckhart, Tolle. 1999. *The power of now: A guide to spiritual enlightenment.* Novato, CA: New World Library. 168-9.

San Jose Insight Meditation Sangha. n.d. *Additional information on Vipassana.* http://www.geocities.com/sjsangha/AdditionalInfo.html (accessed January 1, 2008).

Emerson, Ralph Waldo. n.d. http://en.wikiquote.org/wiki/Ralph_ Waldo_Emerson (accessed January 1, 2008).